Spectrum Test Prep

Grade 4

Test Preparation for:

Reading
Language
Math

Program Authors:
Dale Foreman
Alan C. Cohen
Jerome D. Kaplan
Ruth Mitchell

Copyright © 2001 McGraw-Hill Children's Publishing

Printed in the United States of America. All rights reserved. Except as permitted under the United States Copyright Act, no part of this publication may be reproduced or distributed in any form or by any means, or stored in a database or retrieval system, without prior written permission from the publisher.

Send all inquiries to: McGraw-Hill Children's Publishing • 3195 Wilson Drive NW • Grand Rapids, MI 49544
ISBN: 0-7696-3054-5

2 3 4 5 6 7 8 9 10 PHXBK 07 06 05 04 03

The *McGraw-Hill* Companies

Table of Contents

Test Prep

The Program That Teaches Test-Taking Achievement

For over two decades, McGraw-Hill has helped students perform their best when taking standardized achievement tests. Over the years, we have identified the skills and strategies that students need to master the challenges of taking a standardized test. Becoming familiar with the test-taking experience can help ensure your child's success.

Test Prep covers all test skill areas

Test Prep contains the subject areas that are represented in the five major standardized tests. *Test Prep* will help your child prepare for the following tests:

- California Achievement Tests® (CAT/5)
- Comprehensive Tests of Basic Skills (CTBS/4)
- Iowa Tests of Basic Skills® (ITBS, Form K)
- Metropolitan Achievement Test (MAT/7)
- Stanford Achievement Test(SAT/9)

Test Prep provides strategies for success

Many students need special support when preparing to take a standardized test. *Test Prep* gives your child the opportunity to practice and become familiar with:

- General test content
- The test format
- Listening and following standard directions
- Working in structured settings
- Maintaining a silent, sustained effort
- Using test-taking strategies

Test Prep is comprehensive

Test Prep provides a complete presentation of the types of skills covered in standardized tests in a variety of formats. These formats are similar to those your child will encounter when testing. The subject areas covered in this book include:

- Reading
- Language
- Math

Test Prep gives students the practice they need

Each student lesson provides several components that help develop test-taking skills:

- An **Example,** with directions and sample test items
- A **Tips** feature, that gives test-taking strategies
- A **Practice** section, to help students practice answering questions in each test format

Each book gives focused test practice that builds confidence:

- A **Test Yourself** lesson for each unit gives students the opportunity to apply what they have learned in the unit
- A **Test Practice** section gives students the experience of a longer test-like situation.
- A **Progress Chart** allows students to note and record their own progress.

Test Prep is the first and most successful program ever developed to help students become familiar with the test-taking experience. *Test Prep* can help to build self-confidence, reduce test anxiety, and provide the opportunity for students to successfully show what they have learned.

A Message to Parents and Teachers:

- **Standardized tests: the yardstick for your child's future**

  Standardized testing is one of the cornerstones of American education. From its beginning in the early part of this century, standardized testing has gradually become the yardstick by which student performance is judged. For better or worse, your child's future will be determined in great part by how well he or she performs on the standardized test used by your school district.

- **Even good students can have trouble with testing**

  In general, standardized tests are well designed and carefully developed to assess students' abilities in a consistent and balanced manner. However, there are many factors that can hinder the performance of an individual student when testing. These might include test anxiety, unfamiliarity with the test's format, or failure to understand the directions.

  In addition, it is rare that students are taught all of the material that appears on a standardized test. This is because the curriculum of most schools does not directly match the content of the standardized test. There will certainly be overlap between what your child learns in school and how he or she is tested, but some materials will probably be unfamiliar.

- **Ready to Test will lend a helping hand**

  It is because of the shortcomings of the standardized testing process that *Test Prep* was developed. The lessons in the book were created after a careful analysis of the most popular achievement tests. The items, while different from those on the tests, reflect the types of material that your child will encounter when testing. Students who use *Test Prep* will also become familiar with the format of the most popular achievement tests. This learning experience will reduce anxiety and give your child the opportunity to do his or her best on the next standardized test.

We urge you to review with your child the Message to Students and the feature "How to Use This Book" on pages 8-9. The information on these pages will help your child to use this book and develop important test-taking skills. We are confident that following the recommendations in this book will help your child to earn a test score that accurately reflects his or her true ability.

A Message to Students:

Frequently in school you will be asked to take a standardized achievement test. This test will show how much you know compared to other students in your grade. Your score on a standardized achievement test will help your teachers plan your education. It will also give you and your parents an idea of what your learning strengths and weaknesses are.

This book will help you do your best on a standardized achievement test. It will show you what to expect on the test and will give you a chance to practice important reading and test-taking skills. Here are some suggestions you can follow to make the best use of *Test Prep*.

Plan for success
- You'll do your best if you begin studying and do one or two lessons in this book each week. If you only have a little bit of time before a test is given, you can do one or two lessons each day.
- Study a little bit at a time, no more than 30 minutes a day. If you can, choose the same time each day to study in a quiet place.
- Keep a record of your score on each lesson. The charts on pp. 155 - 157 of this book will help you do this.

On the day of the test . . .
- Get a good night's sleep the night before the test. Have a light breakfast and lunch to keep from feeling drowsy during the test.
- Use the tips you learned in *Test Prep*. The most important tips are to skip difficult items, take the best guess when you're unsure of the answer, and try all the items.
- Don't worry if you are a little nervous when you take an achievement test. This is a natural feeling and may even help you stay alert.

How to Use This Book

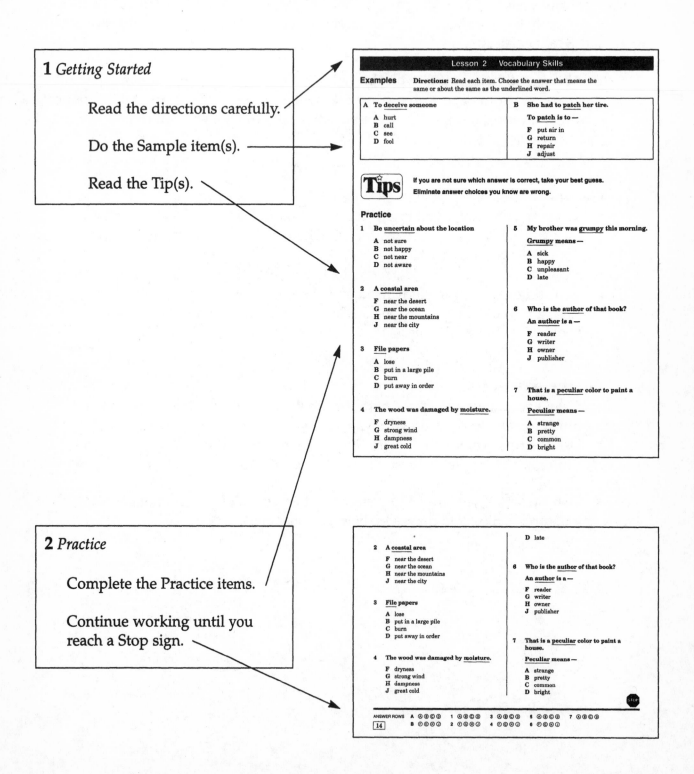

1 *Getting Started*

Read the directions carefully.

Do the Sample item(s).

Read the Tip(s).

2 *Practice*

Complete the Practice items.

Continue working until you reach a Stop sign.

Lesson 2   Vocabulary Skills

Examples   **Directions:** Read each item. Choose the answer that means the same or about the same as the underlined word.

A To deceive someone
   A hurt
   B call
   C see
   D fool

B She had to patch her tire.
   To patch is to —
   F put air in
   G return
   H repair
   J adjust

Tips   If you are not sure which answer is correct, take your best guess. Eliminate answer choices you know are wrong.

Practice

1 Be uncertain about the location
   A not sure
   B not happy
   C not near
   D not aware

2 A coastal area
   F near the desert
   G near the ocean
   H near the mountains
   J near the city

3 File papers
   A lose
   B put in a large pile
   C burn
   D put away in order

4 The wood was damaged by moisture.
   F dryness
   G strong wind
   H dampness
   J great cold

5 My brother was grumpy this morning.
   Grumpy means —
   A sick
   B happy
   C unpleasant
   D late

6 Who is the author of that book?
   An author is a —
   F reader
   G writer
   H owner
   J publisher

7 That is a peculiar color to paint a house.
   Peculiar means —
   A strange
   B pretty
   C common
   D bright

---

2 A coastal area
   F near the desert
   G near the ocean
   H near the mountains
   J near the city

3 File papers
   A lose
   B put in a large pile
   C burn
   D put away in order

4 The wood was damaged by moisture.
   F dryness
   G strong wind
   H dampness
   J great cold

   D late

6 Who is the author of that book?
   An author is a —
   F reader
   G writer
   H owner
   J publisher

7 That is a peculiar color to paint a house.
   Peculiar means —
   A strange
   B pretty
   C common
   D bright

STOP

ANSWER ROWS   A ⒶⒷⒸⒹ   1 ⒶⒷⒸⒹ   3 ⒶⒷⒸⒹ   5 ⒶⒷⒸⒹ   7 ⒶⒷⒸⒹ
14   B ⒡⒢⒣Ⓙ   2 ⒡⒢⒣Ⓙ   4 ⒡⒢⒣Ⓙ   6 ⒡⒢⒣Ⓙ

3 *Check It Out*

Check your answers by turning to the Answer Keys at the back of the book.

Keep track of how you're doing by marking the number right on the Progress Charts on pages 155-157.

Mark the lesson you completed on the Table of Contents for each section.

Answer Keys

Answer Keys						
Reading	1	A	31	B	19	D
Unit 1,	2	J	32	F	20	H
Vocabulary	3	B	33	D	Lesson 11	
Lesson 1	4	G	34	H	E1	C
A C	5	C	35	B	1	D
B H	6	F	Unit 2, Reading		2	H
1 B	Lesson 6		Comprehension		3	C
2 J	A	C	Lesson 8		4	F
3 C	B	F	A	B	5	B
4 F	1	C	1	D	6	F
5 D	2	F	2	F	7	C
6 G	3	B	3	C	8	F
7 A	4	J	4	J	9	D
8 G	5	D	Lesson 9		10	D
Lesson 2	6	H	A	B	11	D
A D	Lesson 7		1	D	12	H
B H	E1	D	2	G	13	B
1 A	E2	H	3	D	14	H
2 G	1	C	4	H	15	A
3 D	2	J	5	B	16	H
4 H	3	C	6	F	17	D
5 C	4	C	7	C	18	G
6 G	5	A	8	F	19	C
7 A	6	H	9	B	20	D
Lesson 3	7	D	10	J	21	D
A A	8	C	11	A	22	H
B J	9	C	12	G	23	D
1 G	10	G	13	C	24	F
2 D	11	B	Lesson 10		25	C
3 F	12	H	A	B	26	G
4 C	13	D	1	B	27	B
5 G	14	F	2	F	28	H
6 A	15	B	3	A	29	A
7 J	16	F	4	H	Test Practice	
8 J	17	F	5	B	Part 1	
Lesson 4	18	J	6	J	E1	D
A A	19	F	7	A	E2	F
B G	20	F	8	F	1	B
1 B	21	C	9	D	2	F
2 J	22	J	10	H	3	A
3 A	23	C	11	B	4	J
4 J	24	H	12	G	5	B
5 A	25	C	13	C	6	H
Lesson 5	26	J	14	J	7	D
A B	27	H	15	C	8	F
B F	28	H	16	G	9	A
	29	G	17	A	10	J
	30	J	18	G	11	C

150

Reading Progress Chart

Circle your score for each lesson. Connect your scores to see how well you are doing.

Unit 1							Unit 2			
Lesson 1	Lesson 2	Lesson 3	Lesson 4	Lesson 5	Lesson 6	Lesson 7	Lesson 8	Lesson 9	Lesson 10	Lesson 11
8	7	8	5	6	6	35 34 33 32 31 30 29 28 27 26 25 24 23 22 21 20 19 18 17 16 15 14 13 12 11 10 9 8 7 6 5 4 3 2 1	4	13 12 11 10 9 8 7 6 5 4 3 2 1	20 19 18 17 16 15 14 13 12 11 10 9 8 7 6 5 4 3 2 1	29 28 27 26 25 24 23 22 21 20 19 18 17 16 15 14 13 12 11 10 9 8 7 6 5 4 3 2 1
7	6	7	4	5	5		3			
6	5	6								
5	4	5	4	4			2			
4		4	3	3	3					
3	3	3	2	2	2		1			
2	2	2								
1	1	1	1	1	1					

155

Table of Contents
Reading

12

Skills

Reading

VOCABULARY

Identifying synonyms
Identifying words with similar meanings
Identifying antonyms
Identifying word meaning from a derivational clue

Identifying multi-meaning words
Identifying words from a defining statement
Identifying words in paragraph context
Identifying affix meaning

READING COMPREHENSION

Recognizing story structures
Differentiating between fact and opinion
Making comparisons
Generalizing from story information
Recognizing details
Understanding events
Drawing conclusions
Applying story information
Deriving word or phrase meaning
Understanding characters
Recognizing the narrator
Using a story web

Sequencing ideas
Making inferences
Predicting from story content
Identifying story genres
Predicting outcomes
Choosing the best title for a passage
Identifying relevant parts of a passage
Understanding the author's purpose
Understanding feelings
Understanding the main idea
Extending a story's meaning

Language Arts

LANGUAGE MECHANICS

Identifying the need for punctuation marks
(period, question mark, exclamation
point, quotation marks, apostrophe,
comma, colon, semicolon) in sentences

Identifying the need for capital letters and
punctuation marks in printed text

LANGUAGE EXPRESSION

Identifying the correct forms of verbs,
adjectives, nouns, and pronouns
Identifying the predicate of a sentence
Identifying correctly formed sentences
Identifying the correct sentence to
complete a paragraph
Sequencing sentences within a paragraph

Recognizing double negatives
Identifying the subject of a sentence
Combining sentences
Identifying sentences that do not fit
in a paragraph
Choosing the right paragraph for a
given purpose

SPELLING

Identifying correctly spelled words

Identifying incorrectly spelled words

STUDY SKILLS

Using an index or table of contents
Understanding an encyclopedia
Understanding a graph
Identifying parts of a book
Using a card catalog

Using a dictionary
Identifying organizational method
Identifying reference sources
Understanding an outline web

Math

CONCEPTS

Associating numerals and number words
Comparing and ordering whole numbers

Comparing and ordering fractions and decimals
Converting between decimals and fractions

Estimating
Finding multiples
Naming numerals
Recognizing odd and even numbers
Reducing fractions
Rounding
Understanding number sentences and
    simple equations
Using a number line
Using expanded notation

Factoring numbers
Identifying fractional parts
Recognizing equivalent fractions
Recognizing visual and numeric patterns
Regrouping
Understanding function tables
Understanding place value
Understanding ratio and proportion
Using a number line with fractions and decimals
Using operational symbols, words, properties

COMPUTATION

Adding whole numbers, decimals,
    and fractions
Multiplying whole numbers

Dividing whole numbers
Subtracting whole numbers, decimals,
    and fractions

APPLICATIONS

Estimating weight and size
Formulating simple number sentences
Reading a calendar
Reading a thermometer
Recognizing plane and solid figures and their
    characteristics
Understanding bar graphs and pictographs
Understanding probability and averages
Using tables and charts
Understanding time concepts
Using standard and metric units of measurement

Finding perimeter and area
Identifying information needed to solve a
    problem
Recognizing value of money and money
    notation
Solving word problems
Understanding parallel lines
Understanding spatial relations, congruence
    and symmetry
Using a coordinate graph

—————— Strategies ——————

Listening carefully
Following group directions
Utilizing test formats
Locating question and answer choices
Following oral directions
Subvocalizing answer choices
Working methodically
Skipping difficult items and returning to them later
Identifying and using key words to find the answer
Staying with the first answer choice
Following complex directions
Trying out answer choices
Eliminating answer choices
Restating a question
Skimming a passage
Using logic
Using context to find the answer
Referring to a passage to find the correct answer
Indicating that an item has no mistakes
Performing the correct operation
Recalling the elements of a correctly
    formed sentence
Converting problems to a workable format
Noting the lettering of answer choices
Taking the best guess when unsure of the answer
Indicating that the correct answer is not given
Identifying the best test-taking strategy
Locating the correct answer
Comparing answer choices

Marking the correct answer as soon as it is found
Adjusting to a structured setting
Maintaining a silent, sustained effort
Managing time effectively
Considering every answer choice
Computing carefully
Checking answer choices
Locating the correct answer
Understanding unusual item formats
Referring to a passage to answer questions
Inferring word meaning from sentence context
Reasoning from facts and evidence
Encapsulating a passage
Responding to items according to difficulty
Avoiding over-analysis of answer choices
Recalling the meaning of familiar words
Ignoring extraneous information
Referring to a reference source
Recalling the elements of a correctly
    formed paragraph
Checking answers by the opposite operation
Finding the answer without computing
Identifying and using key words, figures,
    and numbers
Following written directions
Reworking a problem
Previewing items

Table of Contents
Reading

UNIT 1   VOCABULARY
Lesson 1   Synonyms

Examples   **Directions:** Read each item. Choose the word that means the same or about the same as the underlined word.

A surprising <u>outcome</u>	B To <u>damage</u> a car is to —
A start	F repair
B visit	G buy
C result	H harm
D meaning	J polish

 Be careful. The letters for the answer choices change for each question. Make sure the space you fill in matches the answer you think is correct.

Practice

1 valuable <u>employee</u>

A product
B worker
C boss
D savings

2 <u>tread</u> carefully

F work
G carry
H act
J walk

3 <u>mistaken</u> idea

A super
B accurate
C erroneous
D pleasant

4 <u>observe</u> closely

F watch
G lend
H play
J shoot

5 A <u>jolly</u> person is —

A sad
B tall
C short
D cheerful

6 A <u>brilliant</u> light is —

F distant
G bright
H tiny
J dull

7 An <u>accurate</u> measurement is —

A correct
B incorrect
C large
D difficult

8 To leave <u>hastily</u> is to leave —

F late
G quickly
H slowly
J early

STOP

Examples   **Directions:** Read each item. Choose the answer that means the same or about the same as the underlined word.

A To deceive someone

  A hurt
  B call
  C see
  D fool

B She had to patch her tire.

  To patch is to —

  F put air in
  G return
  H repair
  J adjust

 If you are not sure which answer is correct, take your best guess.

Eliminate answer choices you know are wrong.

Practice

1 Be uncertain about the location

  A not sure
  B not happy
  C not near
  D not aware

2 A coastal area

  F near the desert
  G near the ocean
  H near the mountains
  J near the city

3 File papers

  A lose
  B put in a large pile
  C burn
  D put away in order

4 The wood was damaged by moisture.

  F dryness
  G strong wind
  H dampness
  J great cold

5 My brother was grumpy this morning.

  Grumpy means —

  A sick
  B happy
  C unpleasant
  D late

6 Who is the author of that book?

  An author is a —

  F reader
  G writer
  H owner
  J publisher

7 That is a peculiar color to paint a house.

  Peculiar means —

  A strange
  B pretty
  C common
  D bright

STOP

Examples   **Directions:** Read each item. Choose the word that means the opposite of the underlined word.

A The bowl is **empty**.

A full
B cracked
C small
D heavy

B **original** form

F first
G active
H shallow
J final

 **Tips**   Before you mark your answer, ask yourself: "Does this mean the opposite of the underlined word?"

Practice

1 The trail up the mountain is **difficult**.

(A) challenging
B steep
C easy
D narrow

2 Rain is **possible** today.

F happening
(G) certain
H heavy
J predicted

3 That old couch is **worthless**.

A wonderful
B new
C cherished
D valuable

4 This lake is very **deep**.

(F) shallow
G cold
H large
J warm

5 **recognize** someone

A welcome
B seek
C forget
D hurry

6 very **fortunate**

F charming
G unlucky
H rich
J safe

7 **available** resources

(A) inaccessible
B extra
C recent
D active

8 **branch** office

(F) distant
G large
H whole
J main

ANSWER ROWS
A (A)(B)(C)(D)   1 (A)(B)(C)(D)   3 (A)(B)(C)(D)   5 (A)(B)(C)(D)   7 (A)(B)(C)(D)
B (F)(G)(H)(J)   2 (F)(G)(H)(J)   4 (F)(G)(H)(J)   6 (F)(G)(H)(J)   8 (F)(G)(H)(J)

15

Examples   **Directions:** For items A and 1-2, find the answer in which the underlined word is used the same as in the sentence in the box. For items B and 3-5, read the two sentences with the blanks. Choose the word that fits in both sentences.

A

> **Please turn off the light.**

In which sentence does the word light mean the same thing as in the sentence above?

A The light is too bright in the bedroom.

B The box was light enough to carry.

C You'll need a light jacket.

D The fire is hard to light.

B Someone bought the _____ on the corner.

A new house costs a _____ of money.

F bunch
G lot
H house
J property

 Tips   If a question is too difficult, skip it and come back to it later, if you have time.

Practice

1

> **Write a note to your sister.**

In which sentence does the word note mean the same thing as in the sentence above?

Ⓐ Can you reach that high note?

B This note will explain everything.

C Be sure you note where you parked the car.

D Note how the artist used a mixture of bright and dark colors.

2

> **The first batter hit a home run.**

In which sentence does the word batter mean the same thing as in the sentence above?

F A bumpy car ride will batter you up.

G The cake batter is in the large bowl.

H The kittens love to batter each other around.

Ⓙ Who is the next batter?

3 Inez bought a _____ of soda.

The doctor said it was a difficult _____.

Ⓐ case
B carton
C disease
D situation

4 The _____ is flat.

The runner began to _____.

F turn
G balloon
H lose
Ⓙ tire

5 What _____ does Carl work?

Help me _____ the box to that side.

Ⓐ shift
B time
C move
D job

 STOP

Examples   **Directions:** Read the paragraph. Find the word below the
paragraph that fits best in each numbered blank.

It takes a great deal of _____ **(A)** _____ to become a champion in any

sport. Many hours of practice are _____ **(B)** _____ , and you must often

neglect other aspects of your life.

A A inflammation   B F required
   B dedication   G deflected
   C restriction   H extracted
   D location   J expanded

 Skim the passage first. Then read each sentence with a blank
carefully. Use the meaning of the sentence to find the answer.

Practice

Sometimes the old ways of doing things are still the best. _____ **(1)** _____

many manufactured fibers, for instance, wool and cotton _____ **(2)** _____ the best

materials for making clothes. Wood and bricks, which have been in use for

thousands of years around the world, are the most _____ **(3)** _____ building

materials. When it comes to travel in rugged _____ **(4)** _____ , horses or mules _____ **(5)** _____

any machines we have developed. These examples demonstrate _____ **(6)** _____

that newer isn't always better.

 A Despite   F actions
              B Relying   G terrain
              C Consequently   H accommodations
              D Before   J vehicles

 F eliminate   A elate
              G support   B deny
              H handle   C surpass
              J remain   D enlist

 A unlikely   F conclusively
              B versatile   G rarely
              C responsive   H hopefully
              D motivational   J expressively

STOP

Lesson 6   Word Study

Examples   **Directions:** Read each question. Fill in the circle for the answer
you think is correct.

A Which of these words probably comes from the Latin word *graduare* meaning *to step*? A grand B great C graduate D ingredient	**B** The owner had to _____ the puppy for chewing the shoe. Which of these words means the owner had to speak harshly to the puppy? F scold G pursue H alert J inspire

 **Tips**   If a question sounds confusing, try rephrasing the sentence in a way that is easier to understand.

Mark the right answer as soon as you find it.

Practice

1 Which of these words probably comes from the German word *schnarren* meaning *to growl*?

(A) snap
B shank
C snarl
D strand

2 Which of these words probably comes from the French word *contenir* meaning *to hold*?

F contain
(G) continent
H consent
J conform

3 Our _____ visit to the Grand Canyon took place in 1968.

Which of these words means the visit was our first?

A limited
B initial
(C) sampled
D final

4 Pat was able to _____ the dying plant.

Which of these words means Pat was able to bring the plant back to life?

F elate
G immobilize
H unfurl
(J) revive

For numbers 5 and 6, choose the answer that best defines the underlined part.

5 far**mer**   buil**der**

A place where
B when
C against
(D) person who

6 **pre**pay   **pre**cede

F after
G soon
H before
(J) again

 STOP

ANSWER ROWS   **A** (A)(B)(C)(D)   **1** (A)(B)(C)(D)   **3** (A)(B)(C)(D)   **5** (A)(B)(C)(D)
18   **B** (F)(G)(H)(J)   **2** (F)(G)(H)(J)   **4** (F)(G)(H)(J)   **6** (F)(G)(H)(J)

Examples   Directions: For E1, choose the answer that means the same or about the same as the underlined word. For E2, read the question. Mark the answer you think is correct.

E1 feel grouchy

   A pleasant
   B healthy
   C energetic
   D irritable

E2 Which of these probably comes from the Latin word *magnus* meaning *great*?

   F magnet
   G mangle
   H major
   J minor

For numbers 1-8, find the word or words that mean the same or almost the same as the underlined word.

1 remain stranded

   A crowded
   B open
   C isolated
   D defined

2 claim a right

   F avoid
   G oppose
   H solve
   J demand

3 stitch a shirt

   A buy
   B tear
   C sew
   D lose

4 manage a business

   F quit
   G run
   H join
   J like

5 If something is withered it is —

   A dried up
   B soaked
   C pushed over
   D hidden

6 Final means —

   F next
   G previous
   H last
   J first

7 To purify is to —

   A obtain
   B buy
   C confuse
   D clean

8 This restaurant is very popular.

   F expensive
   G well-liked
   H crowded
   J far away

 GO

For numbers 9-13, find the meaning for each underlined word.

9 The repair to the bridge is supposed to be <u>permanent</u>.

Permanent means —

A temporary
B done quickly
C long-lasting
D inexpensive

10 Your answer is <u>satisfactory</u>, so you passed the test.

Satisfactory means —

F incorrect
G acceptable
H long
J confusing

11 The trail to the lake is <u>incredible</u>.

Incredible means —

A steep
B extraordinary
C long and winding
D boring

12 The dog was <u>filthy</u> after our walk.

Filthy means —

F happy
G clean
H dirty
J tired

13 My cat <u>crouched</u> when she saw the bird.

Crouched means —

A jumped
B ran
C cried loudly
D bent down

For numbers 14-19, find the word that means the opposite of the underlined word.

14 <u>massive</u> rock

F tiny
G gigantic
H balanced
J high

15 a <u>brief</u> visit

A pleasant
B long
C short
D unexpected

16 <u>guided</u> tour

F unassisted
G enjoyable
H expensive
J directed

17 I wonder why he is so <u>timid</u>?

A frightened
B fearless
C cowardly
D angry

18 The museum had a <u>formal</u> luncheon.

F pleasant
G late
H crowded
J casual

19 The package seemed <u>ordinary</u>.

A typical
B original
C unusual
D natural

GO

For numbers 20-23, choose the word that correctly completes both sentences.

20 My _____ is running late.

We will _____ the dog for you.

F watch
G clock
H walk
J find

21 This is a good _____ for a picnic.

There is a _____ on your shirt.

A place
B stain
C spot
D table

22 We caught _____ when we went fishing.

The bird is on its _____ .

F bass
G limb
H trout
J perch

23 The officer was very _____ to me.

This _____ of apple is not so sweet.

A nice
B type
C kind
D friendly

24 Don't forget to put a stamp on the letter.

In which sentence does the word stamp mean the same thing as in the sentence above?

F The secretary used a rubber stamp.
G A horse will often stamp its feet.
H A stamp can only be used once.
J This machine will stamp the part out of a sheet of metal.

25 Where is the sock to match the one on top of the washer?

In which sentence does the word match mean the same thing as in the sentence above?

A The tennis match will begin soon.
B This match will light anywhere there is a rough surface.
C Those two are a match for one another.
D Be sure to match the parts carefully.

For numbers 26 and 27, choose the answer that best defines the underlined part.

26 harmless   needless

F with
G alone
H where
J without

27 impossible   impatient

A too
B so
C not
D of

GO

28 Which of these words probably comes from the Middle English word *fortia* meaning *strong*?

F   former
G   photo
(H) force
J   foreign

29 Which of these words probably comes from the Latin word *socius* meaning *comrade*?

A   sock
B   sociable
(C) solitary
D   song

30 The couple _____ to buy a new house when they could afford it.

Which of these words means the couple meant to buy a house?

F   expanded
(G) released
H   posted
J   intended

31 The ice crystals formed a _____ pattern.

Which of these words means the pattern could be broken easily?

(A) hearty
B   delicate
C   denied
D   duplicate

Read the paragraph. Find the word below the paragraph that fits best in each numbered blank.

A family of owls has made its home in an old barn ___(32)___ to our property. The two adult and two ___(33)___ owls spend most of the day sleeping and only become active around dusk. They hunt most of the night, feeding on mice and rabbits. They appear to be ___(34)___ flyers, but catch their prey without much difficulty. When morning breaks, the family of hunters returns to the ___(35)___ of the old barn.

32 F   adjacent
(G) distant
H   consequent
J   hesitant

33 A   mature
(B) capable
C   responsible
D   juvenile

34 (F) needless
G   partial
H   awkward
J   ancient

35 (A) occasional
B   security
C   annual
D   partially

STOP

Lesson 8   Critical Reading

Example   **Directions:** Read each item. Choose the answer you think is correct. Mark the space for your answer.

The four children sat beside the river and dangled their feet in the water. They had been friends since they had been in kindergarten and did almost everything together. Now that school was finished, they were looking forward to a summer of fun.

A   **What part of a story does this passage tell about?**

  A   The plot
  B   The characters
  C   The mood
  D   The setting

 **Tips**   Read the question and all the answer choices. Once you have decided on the correct answer, ask yourself: "Does this really answer the question?"

Practice

1   Which of these probably came from an ad in the telephone book?

  A   The rain began to fall around noon.

  B   Pablo was sure he could win the race.

  C   The trout is a popular game fish.

  D   We guarantee our work.

2   Julian is reading a story called "Voyage to a New Land."

Which of these sentences is probably the first one in the story?

  F   The family stood on the deck and looked at the land that stretched before them as far as the eye could see.

  G   On calm days, everyone sat on deck enjoying the fresh air and sunshine.

  H   I was too young to remember, but my mother told me about cooking aboard the ship.

  J   It was terribly crowded, with people sleeping anywhere they could find a space.

3   It was going to be a difficult day for the people of Leeds. The huge oak tree in Central Park had been diseased for years, and this was the day it was to be cut down.

What part of a story does this passage tell about?

  A   the plot

  B   the characters

  C   the mood

  D   the setting

4   Which of these sentences states a fact?

  F   Everyone will enjoy visiting our national forests.

  G   The prettiest trees remain green all year long, even in the coldest weather.

  H   The best use of a forest is for recreation.

  J   Trees supply us with food, paper, and wood for building things.

STOP

Example   **Directions:** Read the passage. Find the best answer to each question that follows the passage.

Pizza has sometimes been called "junk food," and in some cases, it really is. When prepared correctly, however, it can be one of the most healthful foods you can eat. A pizza contains nutrients from the major food groups and can easily be made with reduced-fat ingredients.	**A What helps to make pizza a healthful food?** **A** Using ingredients **B** Using low-fat ingredients **C** Using high-fat ingredients **D** Using one of the four food groups

Tips   Look for key words in the question, then find the same words in the passage. This will help you locate the correct answer.

Practice

Here is a passage about a sport that involves real adventure. Read the passage and then do numbers 1 through 7 on page 25.

How is this for adventure? Tie yourself into a tiny boat that can tip over in a flash. Grab a double-headed paddle and set off at breakneck speed down a raging river. Oh, and don't forget your helmet and flotation vest. You'll need both, because an important part of this sport is the guarantee that you'll flip over into chilly water and have to turn yourself back up. If all this sounds wonderful to you, then you should take up the sport of kayaking.

A kayak is a small, enclosed boat that was invented by Native Americans in Alaska and the northern provinces of Canada. They used these seaworthy craft, which were made of animal skins around a wooden frame, to hunt and fish in the ocean, but adventurers today prefer the thrill of shooting the rapids in fiberglass kayaks. Kayaking has grown today into an Olympic sport that is enjoyed by millions of people around the world.

The safest way to learn to kayak is to take lessons. Centers throughout the United States can set you up with an instructor, all the equipment you'll need, and a safe body of water in which to learn. Once you get the hang of kayaking, you can rent equipment and try it on your own in a relatively calm river or lake. Later, as your skills and confidence improve, you can move up to more challenging waters.

It is interesting to note that kayaking can be enjoyed in cities as well as in distant mountain rivers. Even in the large cities in the East, like New York, Philadelphia, and Washington, DC, kayakers are having a ball in local rivers and even the runoff created by heavy storms.

GO

1 The kayak was invented by —

A Canadians.

B modern adventurers.

C residents of cities in the East.

(D) Native Americans.

2 Most kayaks today are made of

F animal skins.

(G) fiberglass.

H wood.

J aluminum.

3 Which of these would be the best title for the passage?

A "The Double Paddle"

B "Adventure in the Ocean"

C "River Fun"

(D) "Old Boat, New Adventure"

4 What does the author mean by the phrase "shooting the rapids"?

F Shooting quickly

(G) Riding a kayak in ocean waves

(H) Riding a kayak down river rapids

J Hunting from a kayak

5 When you kayak down a river, you can almost always expect to —

A be pushed off course by strong winds or ocean currents.

(B) get turned upside-down in the water.

C risk going over a waterfall.

D lose equipment like paddles, helmets, or flotation vests.

6 Which paragraph from the story best supports your answer for number 5?

(F) Paragraph 1

G Paragraph 2

H Paragraph 3

J Paragraph 4

7 The story suggests that once you have learned the basics, you can kayak in more challenging waters.

A word that means the **opposite of** *challenging* is —

A difficult.

B deep.

(C) easy.

D violent.

GO

Mr. Madison's fourth grade class would be leaving soon for their trip to the state capitol. Every year Mr. Madison went through the same preparations and wondered if the weeklong trip each spring was really worth all the work that went into it.

At the beginning of the school year, Mr. Madison talked to his students about the trip and showed them photographs and videos of the fourth grade trip from the year before. He met with the parents of his students to get them involved with planning the trip. He also wanted the parents to have plenty of time to save money for the trip in the spring or to help their son or daughter earn the money needed.

The class would begin immediately to hold car washes, cake sales, and spaghetti dinners to raise money. Everyone in the class was expected to work on at least one project. Mr. Madison and some of the parents found businesses and other people in the community who thought the trip to the state capitol was a good idea. They would be sponsors and donate money to help pay for many of the costs of the trip, such as hiring the bus that would take the class to the state capitol and renting rooms at a nearby hotel.

During the school year, the fourth grade would be learning more about the history of their state. When they went to the capitol in the spring, they would visit some of the places they had learned about and see how their state government worked. But that wasn't all they would do. They would take a ride on a subway, visit an aquarium, go to a skating rink, and even see a major league baseball game. Mr. Madison wanted his students to experience many things that were not available in their small town. He also planned so many activities into each of the four days that everyone would be very tired at the end of each day. Mr. Madison wanted his students to be too exhausted to be thinking up mischief in the middle of the night.

GO

8 In this passage, "sponsors" were people or organizations that —

F contributed money for the trip.

G went to the capitol with the students.

H rented the bus to the students.

J had offices in the capitol.

9 Why did Mr. Madison plan so many activities for each day of the trip?

A So the students wouldn't want to eat too many meals

B To keep the students from getting into trouble at night

C To save money by buying group tickets

D So the sponsors would think the students had a good time

10 Mr. Madison must have thought the trip to the capitol —

F was not worth all the effort.

G was easy to plan because he had done it before.

H was hard to plan because there were so many students.

J was worth all the effort.

11 What is the main reason that Mr. Madison took his class to the state capitol each year?

A So they would learn more than just what was in their books

B As a reward for the hard work the students did all year

C So parents would have a chance to raise money for the trip

D So the students could find sponsors for the trip

12 What does the passage say about where the students lived?

F It was a large city.

G It was a small town.

H It was a suburb of a large city.

J Even though it was a small town, it was the state capitol.

13 Why was the class trip held in the spring?

A The capitol was busier at other times of the year

B The weather in the spring was better than any other time of year

C The students would have most of the school year to prepare for it

D It gave the students a chance to study for final exams

 STOP

Example   **Directions:** Read the passage. Find the best answer to each
question that follows the passage.

Gabby couldn't wait for her parents to get home. They were at the computer store, and she hoped they would bring one home for her. She had asked for a computer often, but the family just couldn't afford one. When her father got a new job, the first thing he did was promise he would get a computer for the children.	**A** **How will Gabby feel if her parents don't come home with a computer?** **A** Angry **B** Disappointed **C** Pleased **D** Confused

 Skim the passage then read the questions. Refer back to the
passage to find the answers. You don't have to reread the story
for each question.

Practice

Here is a passage about someone who did a remarkable deed. Read the passage and then do
numbers 1 through 6 on page 29.

The Hero

Michael hated the building he lived in. His family's apartment was clean and nice inside, but the
outside was dirty and run-down. Trash was everywhere, and all the buildings needed to be painted. He
wished his family could move. Michael wasn't happy sharing a room with his little brother. Joey
whined and cried. He had to go to bed early, and Michael could not do homework or read in their room.
Joey wanted Michael to play with him, and Michael wanted to go outside with his friends. He heard
some neighbors say that someone ought to just set fire to this old building, it was so bad.

One night Michael dreamed that he smelled smoke. He woke up and realized it was no dream. The
building was on fire. He had to climb out the window and save himself. He heard Joey cry out in his
sleep. He heard his father's voice saying, "The fire is in the hall. I can't get to them!"

Michael knew what he had to do. He grabbed some blankets and
wrapped Joey in them. Joey started to cry and call out his name. Michael
talked to Joey and told him not to be afraid. He carefully climbed out of the
burning building and made his way over to the fire escape with the heavy
child in his arms.

When they got to the ground, people were crying and screaming.
Michael handed his brother to a firefighter and sat down on the ground. He
felt very alone and very afraid. Just then his mother and father came up to
the boys and cried and hugged them both. "We thought you were gone. We
couldn't get down the hall," their father said. "Michael, you are a hero for
saving your brother's life."

GO

Michael didn't want to be a hero. He wanted his old apartment back. He wanted his books and toys. He knew how much danger there had been. What if he hadn't been able to get Joey out? Michael didn't feel good at all.

Just then, Michael looked up into the brightest light he had ever seen. A fireman was holding Joey, and a television newswoman was asking Michael how it felt to be a hero. "I don't know," Michael answered quietly. "I just wanted to save my brother."

When the newswoman talked to Michael's parents, they said they didn't care about their things, as long as their boys were all right. They looked at the boys, and Michael looked at his little brother. He knew he had many reasons to feel good about what he had done.

1 Which of these is an *opinion* in the story?

A Joey changed and did not whine and cry any more.

B Michael and several of his neighbors did not like the place they lived.

C Michael's parents tried to save the boys.

D Michael was on the television news.

2 You can tell from the story that Michael—

F really loved his brother.

G was selfish.

H was a coward.

J was a good student in school.

3 At the end of the story, Michael felt—

A happy.

B angry.

C ashamed.

D afraid.

4 This story was probably written to tell about—

F why fire is dangerous.

G how apartment neighbors got a new home.

H how a person did what he had to do.

J why little brothers can be pests.

5 The first paragraph—

A explains how the fire started.

B tells about Michael and his brother.

C describes the furniture in the room.

D introduces Michael's parents.

6 Michael didn't want to play with Joey because—

F he had to do schoolwork instead.

G Joey always wanted to play the same games.

H he didn't like Joey very much.

J he wanted to play with his friends instead.

GO

"Max, get off the couch!" yelled Andy as he and his cousin, Jake, came into the living room.

The big-eared dog opened his eyes and studied the boys for a moment before letting out a long sigh and closing his eyes again.

"MAX!" yelled Andy even louder than before. "GET OFF THE COUCH!"

Max's ears perked up and he opened his eyes, but he stayed in the same spot on the couch watching first one boy and then the other.

"Look, Max, if you get off the couch, I'll get you a dog treat," promised Andy.

Max's tail thumped against the couch, but he didn't move at all.

"Andy, you really have a problem with your dog," said Jake. "He hasn't learned who is the alpha dog in this house."

"What's an alpha dog, Jake? Is that anything like an alphabet?" Andy asked with a grin.

"Well sort of, but you really have to understand how dogs think in order to get them to do what you want. Dogs are members of the same animal family as wolves. Wolves hunt and travel in packs, following a lead wolf who is the strongest male in the pack. When two wolves or dogs meet, the weaker one may lie down and offer his throat. This tells the stronger animal the other one doesn't want to fight. The strongest animal in the pack is known as the alpha, like the letter A. The next strongest is the beta, or letter B, and so on down the line to the weakest animal in the pack," explained Jake.

GO

7 This story web is about the story. Which box contains information that does not belong?

A Box 1

B Box 2

C Box 3

D Box 4

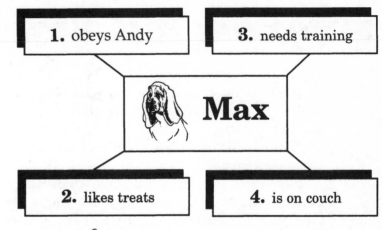

1. obeys Andy

3. needs training

Max

2. likes treats

4. is on couch

8 The main problem with Max was that he —

F only followed commands when he was rewarded.

G couldn't hear Andy's commands so he ignored them.

H was unfriendly to people.

J was on the couch.

9 How does a weaker dog show a stronger dog it doesn't want to fight?

A By barking quietly

B By running away

C By growling then running away

D By appearing defenseless

10 What did Max do when Andy yelled at him?

F He became frightened.

G He jumped off the couch.

H He just looked at Andy.

J He growled at Andy.

11 How can Andy get Max to do as he is told?

A Convince Max that Andy will growl at him

B Convince Max that Andy is the alpha dog

C Make him lie down

D Make Max the alpha dog

12 How does Andy feel when Max won't get off the couch?

F Sad

G Frustrated

H Disappointed

J Worried

13 What happens in a pack of wolves if the alpha wolf disappears?

A An alpha wolf from another pack becomes the leader.

B The wolves fight among themselves.

C The beta wolf becomes the leader.

D The pack also disappears.

GO

Unexpected Visitors

It was a chilly spring morning when Raymond got the surprise of his life. He went outside to put a bag of trash in the can when he saw three bears around the bird feeder. Without thinking, he dropped the bag of trash and rushed back into the house.

"Mom! Dad! Come quick. There are bears outside. They are eating the birdseed. Hurry! What shall we do?"

Raymond's parents rushed to the window and looked outside. Sure enough, a mother bear and her two cubs were nibbling at the birdseed around the ground under the feeder. They seemed quite content and were having a wonderful breakfast.

Just then, Raymond's sisters came down. They looked out the window and jumped back behind their parents.

"Aren't bears dangerous?" asked Merri.

"Not really," answered her mother. "They are shy animals and will usually run away as soon as they know people are around."

"Then why are they so close to the house?" It was Hannah, the youngest sister, and she sounded worried.

"They can't see us," said Mr. Turner. "The bears are just doing what comes naturally, looking for food. The bird seed is a real treat for them."

Just then the mother bear stood up and gave the bird feeder a whack with her paw. The top popped off and all the seeds inside spilled to the ground. The two cubs and the mother began gobbling up the seeds.

"So much for that bird feeder," commented Mrs. Turner.

"It was an old one, and we can buy another. The feed store has a new type that is bearproof. We can hang it higher so the bears can't reach it. I don't mind losing the feeder to the bears this time. How many people in New Jersey get to see bears in their backyard?"

The family stood at the window for a few minutes, watching the bears. They finished up the seed and looked around for other things to eat. Finding nothing, the mother bear made a growling sound and started walking off. The two cubs followed her, tumbling over one another playfully, but always keeping up with the mother. In a moment, they disappeared into the woods.

"Boy," giggled Raymond, "am I going to have a great story for the kids in school!"

14 In this story, Hannah sounds —

F disappointed.

G excited.

H angry.

J concerned.

15 Which of these events will most likely happen after the end of this story?

A Raymond will burn the trash.

B Hannah will always be afraid of bears and other animals.

C Raymond will pick up the bag of trash he dropped.

D Merri will write a story about the bears.

16 How did the mother bear signal to the cubs?

F By picking them up in her mouth

G By growling

H By sniffing at them

J By licking them

17 From this story, you learn that —

A bears and people are afraid of one another.

B bears aren't afraid of people.

C people aren't afraid of bears.

D bears are afraid of houses.

18 This story is mostly about —

F the life of bears.

G an unexpected encounter.

H what bears eat.

J a boy getting ready for school.

19 From this story, you can conclude that —

A bears are seen by many people in New Jersey.

B bears and birds are enemies.

C Mr. Turner was angry that the bear damaged the bird feeder.

D not many people in New Jersey see bears in their backyard.

20 When Raymond tells this story to his friends at school, they will probably —

F believe him right away because this is a common happening.

G go home and look for bears at their own bird feeders.

H doubt it really happened to him because the story is unusual.

J doubt any other story Raymond tries to tell them.

STOP

Example   Directions: Read the passage. Find the best answer to the question that follows the passage.

It was a bright, sunny day, and Rosa was enjoying the beach with her family. Early in the afternoon, however, clouds began building up in the west. Soon they had moved closer and a cool wind started blowing. Mr. Gomez suggested that the family get everything together in case they had to leave quickly.

A   Mr. Gomez wanted everyone to get ready because —

A   it was getting too hot.
B   the beach was crowded.
C   he expected a storm.
D   the water was too cold.

Read the title to the story and then the story. Read each question on the next page and choose the answer you think is best. Mark the space for your answer.

Weather Makers

Our earth is often surrounded by clouds. If we could look down from a spaceship, we would see bands of gray streaks and mounds that look like fluffy cotton. Some might be like thin strips of spider webs.

The clouds that usually bring rain are called nimbus clouds. They are large and dark, and often rise high into the sky.

The wispy, light clouds that appear very high in the sky are called cirrus clouds. Sometimes called horsetails, they appear when the weather is about to change from fair to stormy.

Cumulus clouds are large, white, and puffy, and look very much like cotton balls. They appear on fair days, but can sometimes form thunderheads on hot, moist days.

Clouds are made up of water vapor. They form when water on the earth evaporates and changes to a gas in the air. This water comes from lakes, rivers, and oceans. When the water vapor rises to where it cools, it mixes with tiny pieces of dust to form clouds.

As the water vapor in the clouds rises higher, it gets cooler. The higher it gets, the cooler it gets. When the water vapor cools down enough, the cloud gives up some of its water. Cooler air cannot hold as much water as warm air, so the water falls back to earth in the form of rain.

Clouds protect the earth in two ways. In the summer, clouds help keep the temperature cooler. In the winter, clouds help keep the earth warmer. Summer days are hotter when there are no clouds. Winter days are colder when there are no clouds. Clouds act like a blanket over the earth. Clouds keep the water moving from earth to sky and back to earth again. By "making weather," clouds help keep the earth from becoming too wet or too dry and too hot or too cold.

GO

1 **If the writer were to add to this story, which of these would fit best?**

A How a plane flew into a cloud and an adventure started

B Artists who liked to draw clouds

C Making decorative clouds with cotton

D How people can seed clouds to make it rain

2 **After water vapor rises from the earth and forms clouds, what happens next?**

F The air on earth gets cooler.

G Lightning and thunder appear several hours later.

H Clouds rise higher, become cooler, and dump rain back on earth.

J The air on earth gets warmer.

3 **Clouds are mostly —**

A dust.

B blowing snow.

C water vapor.

D foam.

4 **After reading the passage, you might compare clouds to —**

F using an umbrella for shade.

G filling a bucket of water.

H watering a lawn.

J climbing a tall tree.

5 **If there were no clouds, the earth would be —**

A warmer in winter and cooler in summer.

B cooler in winter and warmer in summer.

C warmer all the time.

D cooler all the time.

6 **The fifth paragraph is mainly about —**

F how clouds are formed.

G why clouds are important on the earth.

H what clouds look like.

J what causes fog.

GO

Speedy Makes a Friend

"This looks like a safe place," Speedy said to himself. Then he scurried under the barn and looked around a bit. He had been in his family's nest in a field when a farmer started plowing the ground. All the rabbits ran in different directions. Speedy didn't even know where the others were, but he was almost grown anyway. He was ready to go out on his own and live his own life.

Right outside the barn was a nice vegetable garden. Green plants were lined up in rows, so he would have plenty to eat. Beside the garden was a nice lawn with delicious grass. Speedy had just stepped out from under the barn to visit the garden when he saw an enormous, black dog. He was so scared that he dove under the barn as fast as he could. The dog, however, did not growl or chase him. The next day he let the dog see him, but stayed close to the barn. Then he slowly hopped out, and the dog did not seem to care about him at all. Speedy felt safe. He even drank water from the big dog's dish, but only when the dog was not around.

Speedy was really happy in his new home when, one day, four other dogs came running up and chased him around the yard. He barely made it back to safety. He would have to watch out for them in the future!

One day, the big dog was in the yard looking for something. "Have you seen my bone, Rabbit? I know I left it here. Oh, there it is, under the barn. I can't reach it." He tried to get it with his paw and his mouth, but he was too big.

Speedy tried to help. He pushed on the bone and was finally able to kick it out to where the dog could reach it. "Thanks, Rabbit," said the big, black dog. "Someday, maybe I can do you a favor."

A few days later, Speedy was careless. He was in the garden eating juicy carrot tops when the pack of dogs came back. He was surrounded by angry dogs with no place to run. "I've had it this time," Speedy thought to himself. "There's no way out."

Just then he heard a huge, deep bark. It was the big, black dog. He came up to the other dogs and let out a growl that showed he meant business. The other dogs took off and never even looked back. Speedy looked at the big dog and let out a big sigh. He hopped up to the big dog, rubbed against him, and said, "Thanks, Big Dog."

GO

7 What did Speedy find out through this experience?

  A Never trust a dog.

  B Do not eat carrots from a vegetable garden.

  C Doing good deeds can pay off in the future.

  D There's no place like home.

8 This story is *mostly* about a rabbit who —

  F found a home and a friend.

  G did something foolish.

  H had only bad things happen to him.

  J was chased out of the vegetable garden.

9 Why did Speedy come to live under the barn?

  A He was tired of his old home.

  B Dogs chased him away from his old home in the field.

  C He had to leave home because he was grown.

  D His old home had been destroyed.

10 What words in the story show that Speedy felt safe in his new home?

  F He even drank water from the big dog's dish...

  G Speedy tried to help.

  H Green plants were lined up in rows...

  J The next day he let the dog see him...

11 This story is most like a —

  A true story.

  B fairy tale.

  C mystery.

  D folktale.

12 When Speedy first met Big Dog, he probably felt —

  F comfortable.

  G angry.

  H frightened.

  J foolish.

13 What will probably happen next?

  A Speedy will find his family and go away with them.

  B Big Dog and Speedy will become good friends.

  C The pack of dogs won't come back to the garden.

  D Big Dog and Speedy will have other adventures.

GO

Joseph and the Cactus

Joseph and his family were on vacation in Mexico. They had visited the markets, explored ancient ruins, and had gone fishing. It was an exciting and fun vacation.

One day, they drove out into the desert. They went in the early morning and made sure they took a shade tent with them, as well as plenty of water. Joseph had read about cactus at school for a report and wanted to see as many as he could. He knew that there are over 2,000 kinds of cactus. More kinds of cactus grow in Mexico than anywhere else. He wanted to dig one up and take it home with him.

Even early in the day, it was growing hot as Joseph and his family admired the beautiful cactus flowers. "They don't look like any other flowers I've ever seen," said his mother. His younger sister added, "Red, yellow, orange, purple, white, brown, pink. Look at all the different colors."

Joseph remembered his report and explained that, "Most cactus blossoms do not last long. Did you know that cactus have fruit, also? Some people say all cactus fruit can be eaten. The birds like the fruit and even the flesh of the plant. Did you know that if a person was without water in the desert he could break open a piece of cactus and get the water stored inside?"

"Ouch! You would have to get past those awful stickers first," laughed his sister.

"Ranchers sometimes burn the spines off and feed the cactus to their cattle when it is really dry and there is no grass for them," Joseph told his family. "The cattle seem to enjoy it."

"I'm glad you studied about cactus," his father said, "but I think we had better have a cool drink and then head back to town. Did you find a cactus to take home, Son?"

"No, they are so beautiful here in their natural home, I'm just going to take some pictures. I'm not sure that the people would let me carry it across the border anyway. The spines would be a problem. I'd rather remember the cactus the way they are here, with the sand, the blossoms, and the mountains in the distance," he answered.

GO

14 What purpose do the spines on cactus serve?

    F Attracting bees to the plant

    G Saving water for the plant

    (H) Protecting the plant from animals

    J Making the plant beautiful

15 What will probably happen next?

    (A) The family will continue their vacation trip.

    B Joseph will change his mind and dig up the cactus.

    C A big rainstorm will come.

    D The family will walk back to their hotel at the beach.

16 The boxes show some things that happened in the story.

Joseph and his family drove into the desert.		His sister found out about the stickers.
1	2	3

Which of these belongs in Box 2?

    F Joseph read about cactus for a school project.

    (G) Joseph told the family about cactus.

    H Joseph decided not to dig up a cactus and bring it home.

    J The family headed back to the hotel.

17 Why did Joseph decide not to dig up a cactus to take home?

    A It was too hot to dig out in the sun then.

    B His sister begged him not to do it.

    C It was against the law to dig up cactus.

    (D) He decided it belonged in the desert.

18 Which of these would *most* help a reader understand the story?

    F Looking up the word "cactus" in a dictionary

    (G) Going to the desert or botanical garden to see cactus in bloom

    H Watching television programs about the desert

    (J) Talking with friends who have been to the desert

19 Which word best describes Joseph's day?

    A Confusing

    B Exhausting

    (C) Enjoyable

    D Dangerous

Prickly Pear Cactus

Fruit

Spines

Paddle

GO

Is this a picnic?

On Friday afternoon, Marta hurried home from school. The other children were planning picnics, trips, or other things for the weekend. Their plans sounded wonderful, and Marta wished she could do similar things. Marta did not look forward to the weekend. She and her family worked very hard all weekend. Marta was glad for Monday morning to come so she could go back to school.

Marta's family worked picking fruit and vegetables for farmers in the valley near their home. At winter harvest time, there was always more work to be done than there were workers. Marta's father explained that everyone had to help so that the family could buy the things they needed.

On Saturday, Marta's job was to watch the baby and to help pick fruit on low branches. The sun would be hot before the day was over. Marta had to move the baby to be sure he was in the shade. She had to give him his bottle. She was sure every girl in her fourth grade class had more wonderful things to do today than watch a baby and pick oranges.

The family came back to the truck at lunchtime. Marta's mother spread out the picnic on a cloth. The family ate the delicious food that she had made. The grown-ups lay down on the blankets in the shade and rested and played with the baby. Marta's brothers tossed a baseball for a while and then sat with them. Marta's mother and father told stories about life long ago. Marta loved hearing the stories. After a while, everyone ate some of the sweet, delicious oranges just off the trees. Then they returned to their harvest.

When they finished on Sunday evening, Marta smiled and remembered the stories and the food. It was fun to have the whole family together, and the work wasn't really that hard. Her father had said they would earn hundreds of dollars for their work. The family would be able to go shopping later for new clothes and things for the house. That would be a good time for everyone. "We really did go out to the country and have a family picnic," Marta thought. "We just did things that other people don't do. Besides, we got paid for our picnic."

GO

20 How did Marta's feelings change from the beginning of the story to the end?

F   She was happy at first and happier later.

(G) She was unhappy at first and happy later.

H   She was happy at first and disappointed later.

J   She was unhappy at first and angry later.

21 Which of these probably happened after the story ended?

A   Marta became a farmer when she grew up.

(B) The family went to a mall.

C   Her brothers quit school to go to work.

D   Marta told her friends at school a story about her weekend.

22 What lesson does this story teach?

F   The best way to have fun is to work with your family.

G   A fourth grader is too young to watch a baby.

(H) Families can have fun together, even when they are working.

J   Parents should not make their children work.

23 What time of year did the story take place?

(A) Spring

(B) Summer

C   Fall

D   Winter

24 In the story, Marta did all of these *except* —

(F) prepare lunch.

G   watch the baby.

H   pick oranges.

J   have a picnic.

25 At lunchtime, which of these happened?

A   Marta's father played the guitar and sang.

B   Marta's mother took a nap under an orange tree.

(C) Marta's brothers played ball.

D   Marta read a book.

GO

For numbers 26 through 29, choose the best answer to the question.

26 Which of these sentences about a new breakfast cereal is not an opinion?

F   Snappies taste better than the cereal you eat now.

G   A box of Snappies contains 16 ounces of cereal.

H   Snappies will help you stay happy the whole day.

J   People who eat Snappies enjoy themselves better than those who don't.

27 Raquel is reading a story called "The Mystery of the House on the Hill."

Which of these sentences is probably the last one in the story?

A   Everyone in town was certain the old Sanford house was haunted.

B   With the mystery solved, Clyde left the house with his friends and headed back down the hill.

C   They quietly walked up the steps and looked in the window.

D   The basement door was open slightly, and they were sure that the noise they heard was coming from behind the door.

28 Which of these sentences states an opinion?

F   There are fifty states in the United States.

G   The largest state is Alaska, and the smallest is Delaware.

H   The people in Kansas work harder than those in Nebraska.

J   The Colorado River provides water to the people in many western states.

29 Which of these statements describes the setting for a story?

A   A stream flowed through the desert canyon, providing the moisture needed for plants and animals to thrive.

B   Coyotes often travel in packs and sometimes begin to howl for no apparent reason.

C   When the Steen family left St. Louis, they had no idea how difficult their trip to California would be.

D   Everyone was overjoyed when they discovered the stream flowing out of the desert canyon.

STOP

UNIT 3   TEST PRACTICE

Part 1   Vocabulary

Examples   **Directions:** For E1, choose the answer that means the same or about the same as the underlined word. For E2, read the question. Mark the answer you think is correct.

E1 nearby store

   A busy
   B distant
   C expensive
   D close

E2 Which of these probably comes from the Old English word *seldum* meaning *infrequent*?

   F seldom
   G insulted
   H salad
   J similar

For numbers 1-8, find the word or words that mean the same or almost the same as the underlined word.

1 need desperately

   A slowly
   B urgently
   C openly
   (D) formally

2 vanquished army

   (F) beaten
   G victorious
   H resting
   J active

3 investigate a mystery

   (A) look into
   B create
   C be frightened by
   D enjoy

4 gather information

   F lost
   G distribute
   H hide
   (J) collect

5 To be ridiculous is to be —

   A sensible
   (B) foolish
   C confusing
   D pleasant

6 To arrive promptly is to be —

   F late
   G by car
   (H) on time
   J with friends

7 If something is superb it is —

   (A) not acceptable
   B worse than average
   C average
   D better than average

8 You will really enjoy this novel.

   F long book
   (G) short book
   H long vacation
   J short vacation

GO

9   The teacher made a just decision.

    Just means —

    A   fair
    B   quick
    C   bad
    D   unexpected

10 Casey completed every detail of the project.

    A detail is a —

    F   step
    G   major component
    H   form
    J   small item

11 The snow on the mountain gradually disappeared.

    Gradually means —

    A   never
    B   all at once
    C   little by little
    D   hardly

12 Fran felt bashful in front of the class.

    To be bashful is to be —

    F   moody
    G   shy
    H   forward
    J   confused

13 Kayla dismounted and walked around the horse.

    Dismounted means—

    A   got off
    B   rode on
    C   ran up
    D   got on

For numbers 14-19, find the word that means the opposite of the underlined word.

14 monopolize the phone

    F   use
    G   lose
    H   repair
    J   share

15 lively discussion

    A   long
    B   short
    C   dull
    D   angry

16 the simple design

    F   colorful
    G   complicated
    H   unusual
    J   plain

17 a harsh tone of voice

    A   shrill
    B   pleasant
    C   quiet
    D   rude

18 Ted was definitely going with us.

    F   possibly
    G   surely
    H   thoroughly
    J   lately

19 Our old car is still reliable.

    A   dependable
    B   broken
    C   missing
    D   undependable

GO

For numbers 20-23, choose the word that correctly completes both sentences.

20 On which _____ will you go to the hospital?

Have you ever tasted a _____ ?

F day
G date
H plum
J appointment

21 It must feel terrible to _____ someone from a job.

The _____ will keep us warm.

A chase
B oven
C dismiss
D fire

22 You will need a _____ to dig a hole in hard dirt.

Which pair of shoes did you _____ ?

F shovel
G pick
H choose
J buy

23 How long will the play _____ ?

This is the _____ bottle of milk.

A take
B only
C last
D continue

24

> The children sat on the step.

In which sentence does the word step mean the same thing as in the sentence above?

F The first step involves cutting the fruit into pieces.

G Don't step on that piece of glass.

H Each step up the steep hill became more difficult.

J The front step was covered with snow.

25

> The mayor will address the town council.

In which sentence does the word address mean the same thing as in the sentence above?

A Address her with the respect due her office.

B This is the wrong street address.

C Remember the zip code when you address the letter.

D In golf, you must address the ball carefully.

For numbers 26 and 27, choose the answer that best defines the underlined part.

26 submarine   subnormal

F below
G around
H since
J above

27 harder   taller

A less
B again
C more
D never

47

GO

28 Which of these words probably comes from the Old French word *gentil* meaning *noble*?

   F   generate
   G   gland
   H   gentle
   J   glisten

29 Which of these words probably comes from the Greek word *phasis* meaning *appearance*?

   A   fail
   B   phantom
   C   phrase
   D   phase

30 A _____ storm blew down trees and power lines around our house.

Which of these words means the storm was very strong?

   F   violent
   G   talented
   H   pleasant
   J   subjected

31 Monica found a _____ necklace at a garage sale.

Which of these words means Monica found a necklace that is worth a lot?

   A   exploded
   B   exaggerated
   C   minimized
   D   valuable

Read the paragraph. Find the word below the paragraph that fits best in each numbered blank.

Young people today have an ___(32)___ future ahead of them. In just a few years, they will see a new ___(33)___ arrive as we leave the 1900s and enter the 2000s. Our world will be a very different place because of ___(34)___ in technology, communication, and transportation. Medical science will ___(35)___ life and let us enjoy active lives much longer. Perhaps the most remarkable trend the future holds is the possibility of traveling to the moon and Mars.

32 F   awful
   G   unkind
   H   exciting
   J   opportunity

33 A   moment
   B   century
   C   guarantee
   D   sentiment

34 F   expenses
   G   deterioration
   H   reflections
   J   advances

35 A   prolong
   B   finance
   C   adhere
   D   standardize

STOP

Example   Directions: Read the passage. Find the best answer to the question that follows the passage.

E1

Ever since he was a child, Roberto wanted to play professional baseball. He practiced almost every day, played whenever he could, and read about all the great players. While he was in high school, Roberto achieved his dream and was chosen by a professional team. To everyone's surprise, he turned the offer down. He wanted to attend college first before he made baseball his career.

A What do you think will most likely happen after Roberto finishes college?

A He will play another professional sport.

B He will write books about baseball.

C He will play professional baseball.

D He will coach basketball.

Here is a passage about an activity that many Americans enjoy. Read the passage and then do numbers 1 through 7 on page 50.

Nothing symbolizes summer in America more than cooking over a grill. In almost every American home, summer holidays are celebrated with a "cookout" in the backyard, on the deck, or anywhere a grill can be set up. The smell of sizzling food on a warm breeze is one of the memories of summer all of us remember fondly on cold winter days.

The word "barbecue" is sometimes used to describe food that is cooked on a grill. Its use can be confusing, however, because "barbecue" has several other meanings. Meat cooked over or in an open pit of coals is considered barbecue, as is meat that is slowly roasted in an oven or simmered in a sauce. Whatever you call it—grilled or barbecued—food cooked over an open flame has a special flavor that normal food lacks.

Traditional cookout fare is the hot dog and hamburger. Steaks are served on special occasions, and for people trying to cut the fat out of their diet, chicken and fish can be cooked on the grill.

Many people are surprised to learn that vegetables can be prepared deliciously on a grill. Potatoes develop an exciting new flavor when cooked on a grill, as do corn, peppers, and onions. Tomatoes, mushrooms, and squash can also be grilled, but they take a little more effort than firmer vegetables. These soft vegetables can be easily overcooked, and they will fall through the spaces in the grill.

The simplest grilling is done over charcoal that has been burned until it is red-hot. For added taste, wood chips from oak, mesquite, or other trees can be added to the charcoal. The most convenient grills burn a gas, like propane, that heats special rocks made from volcanic lava. Gas grills are among the most popular because they are so simple to use and heat quickly to cooking temperature.

1   According to this passage, which of
    these is a soft vegetable?

    A   Tomatoes

    B   Potatoes

    C   Peppers

    D   Onions

2   Which of these is the best title for the
    passage?

    F   "Delicious Foods"

    G   "Four Ways to Cook Food"

    H   "The Great American Cookout"

    J   "Meats and Vegetables"

3   According to the passage, which of
    these foods is lowest in fat?

    A   Hot dogs

    B   Steaks

    C   Chicken

    D   Hamburgers

4   Which of these is not an advantage of
    cooking on a gas grill?

    F   Convenience

    G   Quick heating

    H   Traditional barbecue flavor

    J   Wood flavor

5   What does the word "fare" mean in the
    phrase "traditional cookout fare"?

    A   Open pit cooking

    B   Food

    C   Flavor

    D   Mesquite grilling

6   This passage suggests that—

    F   food cooked over a grill is better for you
        than food cooked in an oven.

    G   it is difficult to cook vegetables on a
        barbecue grill.

    H   cooking over a grill is something many
        Americans enjoy.

    J   slow roasting is the best way to prepare
        meat and vegetables.

7   Many people are _____ that some
    vegetables can be cooked on a grill.

    Which of these words indicates that
    many people don't know about cooking
    vegetables on a grill.

    A   unaware

    B   satisfied

    C   confident

    D   relieved

GO

Read the passage and questions. Choose the answer that is better than the others.

In New York Harbor stands one of the most recognized figures in the world, the Statue of Liberty. This 150-foot tall statue, a gift from the people of France to the American people, honored the 1876 Centennial celebration, America's one hundredth birthday.

The statue, a creation of Frederic Auguste Bartholdi, was first assembled in Paris in 1884. It has a wrought-iron framework designed by Gustave Eiffel, who also designed the Eiffel Tower in Paris. After being assembled, it was disassembled and shipped across the Atlantic Ocean. The Statue of Liberty was then completely reassembled on a base planned by Richard Morris Hunt, a noted American architect.

The Statue of Liberty and its base were paid for in an unusual way, without government help. Instead, the people of France made contributions for the statue, and the people of America made contributions for the base. Among the contributors were many school children, who took great pride in knowing that their pennies helped to build such a wonderful monument.

Even though the outside of the Statue of Liberty is made of copper, it does not appear copper colored. Exposure to the air over the years has turned the skin a bluish-green color, which is known as verdigris.

On October 26, 1886, the Statue of Liberty was unveiled in its permanent location in New York Harbor. On its base was a plaque with a poem written by Emma Lazarus welcoming immigrants to the new land. Two lines near the end of the poem summarizes the statue's spirit: "Give me your tired, your poor, your huddled masses yearning to breathe free." Thousands of people were at the unveiling, and since then, millions have visited this symbol of freedom.

GO

8 **What makes the Statue of Liberty different from many other monuments?**

F   It celebrated freedom.

G   It was paid for by the people of two countries, not the government.

H   It was much taller than any other monument.

J   It was made by a French sculptor.

9 **Based on what you read in the passage, when was the United States "born?"**

A   1776

B   1876

C   1884

D   1886

10 **Why did school children feel proud of the Statue of Liberty?**

F   They contributed money to help build the statue.

G   They contributed money to help ship the statue to the United States.

H   They had a contest to pick the poem for the base.

J   They contributed money to help build the base.

11 **Who planned the base on which the Statue of Liberty stands?**

A   Gustave Eiffel

B   Richard Hunt

C   Frederic Bartholdi

D   Emma Lazarus

12 **Why did the Statue of Liberty have to be disassembled so it could be shipped to America?**

F   It was too large for any ship at the time to carry it.

G   The copper skin was beginning to turn green.

H   It was a gift to the American people for the Centennial.

J   The people of Paris wanted to see it first.

13 **Why do you think the poem by Emma Lazarus was chosen for the plaque on the Statue of Liberty?**

A   Emma Lazarus was a famous American poet.

B   The poem and the statue both welcomed immigrants.

C   It refers to the people of France who gave the statue to America.

D   No one else wanted to write a poem about the statue.

GO

The Hardest Thing Ever

"This is a big commitment, kids. You'll have to help take care of the puppy and train her. Most of all, you'll have to be willing to give her up in a year."

When Mom said that, I really didn't think very much about it. I was too excited to be getting our first puppy. But today I really understand what she meant. Giving up Rachel was the hardest thing ever.

The day we picked Rachel up was one of the best in my life. My sister, Tina, and I raced from the car into the kennel. Mrs. Harbison was waiting for us, and on a leash beside her was the cutest, blackest, Labrador retriever I'd ever seen. We knelt down beside her and she licked our faces, nibbled our ears, and rolled over on her back between us. It was love at first sight for all of us.

On the way home from the kennel, Dad reminded us what we were doing. "Rachel isn't our dog forever, kids. We can keep her for only one year. Our job is to help Rachel get used to people and to give her basic training. A year from now, we have to return her to Mrs. Harbison so she can begin Rachel's real training as a guide dog. Someday, Rachel will become the guide and companion for a blind person. Rachel will do one of the most important jobs in the world."

To be honest, I heard every word Dad said and tried to believe him. I guess my head was thinking about what he said, but my heart didn't understand a word of it.

Every day, Rachel became more a part of our lives. She whined goodbye when we left for school in the morning and was waiting at the door when we returned. She slept in my room, but every once in a while wandered into Tina's room, just to check up on her. Rachel loved Mom and Dad, too, but it was clear she was my dog.

"Don't forget, Eddie, Rachel is only ours for a year. You can love her as much as you want, but we have to give her up next year." Mom and Dad must have said this a thousand times, and every time I nodded my head. My heart, however, still didn't believe it.

The months went by, and Rachel grew into a big dog. She went swimming with me, chased sticks and balls, and learned how much fun the snow could be. Our cat, Patches, even fell in love with Rachel. Whenever Rachel curled up for a nap, Patches would run right over and snuggle up between her legs.

It was a rainy day in November when we had to bring Rachel back to Mrs. Harbison. I thought I was going to die. On the way to the kennel, Rachel sat between Tina and me as if she knew what was happening. When we arrived at the kennel, I wasn't sure I could even get out of the car.

Then something happened that made me feel a little better. Mrs. Harbison walked over to the car with a young woman holding her arm. We could see that she was blind.

"This is Lauren Wolf. She and Rachel will be trained together. When they have finished their training, Rachel will be Lauren's dog."

I never got over losing Rachel, not until last week. We received an invitation to Rachel's graduation from guide dog school. At first, I didn't want to go, but my folks talked me into it. I'm glad they did. When I saw Rachel and Lauren, I knew we had done the right thing. Rachel remembered me, but it was clear she was Lauren's dog now. I could also see that Lauren had a better life because of Rachel. A year ago, Lauren often needed help getting around. Today, she moved around confidently and capably. Through Rachel, we had helped Lauren become a fully independent person.

On the way home, I said something I thought I never would. I asked Mom and Dad if we could get another guide dog.

14 Who is telling this story?

   F Mom   **H** Tina

   G Dad   **J** Eddie

15 What was the "hardest thing"?

   A giving up Rachel   **C** meeting Lauren Wolf

   B training Rachel   **D** going to Rachel's graduation

16 In this story, Eddie learns that —

   F it is important to listen to parents, even if you don't like what they say.

   G doing the right thing can often be difficult.

   H raising a puppy is harder work than it looks.

   J dogs usually like one person in a family more than the others.

17 Which of these describes how Eddie's feelings changed during the story?

   A He was happy for a year, then was sad, and never became happy again.

   B He was happy for a year, then was angry when he had to give up Rachel.

   C He was happy for a year, then was sad, and eventually became happy again.

   D At first he was happy, but became sad and never wanted a dog again.

GO

STRAWBERRIES

Almost everyone likes strawberries. They are sweet, juicy, and good for you, too. They contain more vitamin C than oranges or grapefruit, and are high in fiber. Strawberries grow in the wild where they have very sweet fruit. Birds love them, but they are so small people don't often eat them. Strawberries from a home garden are much bigger. They grow on a small vine that bears fruit after it is at least two years old.

Because they spoil easily, strawberries must be kept cool. They used to be a rare treat, but they are widely available in stores year-round now because refrigerated planes, trains, and trucks can carry them from farms around the country or the world to your local market.

People who need to be careful about eating too much sugar can enjoy strawberries. A whole cup of strawberries has about the same number of calories and natural fruit sugar as a half cup of many other fruits.

If you want to cut down on the amount of sugar you eat and still enjoy a sweet treat, here is a delicious, sugarless, strawberry jam you can make for the family.

You will need:
- 2 cups strawberries, washed, sliced, with green caps removed (or use frozen ones, without sugar)
- 1/4 cup frozen pineapple juice concentrate, thawed
- 1 cup mashed banana (mash ripe banana with a fork)
- 3 tablespoons cornstarch
- 3 tablespoons cold water

Mix strawberries, with their juice, and pineapple juice concentrate. Microwave on high for one minute. Stir mashed banana until it is creamy. Mix into strawberries and juice.

Combine cornstarch and water in a small bowl. Add to strawberries. Stir well. Microwave on high for 30 seconds. Stir. Microwave on high for 30 seconds. Stir. Continue until the jam is thick and is dark red. Cool. Store in refrigerator.

For family members who are not watching their sugar or calories, this jam would be good over ice cream or pound cake.

18 **Which of these is a fact stated in the article?**

F Wild strawberries are very sweet.

G The sugarless strawberry jam is delicious.

H Almost everyone likes strawberries.

J Strawberries grow on a small vine.

19 **How old must strawberry plants be before they bear fruit?**

A Three years

B Six months

C Two years

D One year

20 **Strawberries contain—**

F many vitamins and fewer calories than other fruit.

G many calories and fewer vitamins than other fruit.

H few calories and few vitamins.

J many calories and many vitamins.

21 **People can enjoy strawberries more now than they could years ago because —**

A there are more strawberry farms now than earlier.

B refrigerated transportation gets the berries to market more quickly.

C new varieties of strawberries have been developed.

D now people know more about how to make jam and other dishes.

22 **When you are making the jam, you must put it in the microwave and cook it, stir it, and then —**

F repeat the cooking and stirring until it is thick and dark.

G freeze the jam.

H stir it while the jam is cooking in the microwave.

J add sugar until it tastes good.

23 **The information in this article was written in order to —**

A explain how to grow strawberries.

B get the reader to eat healthful fruits and vegetables.

C tell about strawberries and provide a tasty recipe.

D get the reader to eat foods that have fewer calories.

GO

For numbers 24 through 27, choose the best answer to the question.

24   Robert lived with his father in a trailer near the river. The two of them spent every spare minute fishing or boating in the river. That's how they met Mrs. Herera, an energetic woman of 92 years who shared their love of the river.

What part of a story does this passage tell about?

F The plot

G The characters

H The mood

J The setting

25 **Which of these sentences states an opinion?**

A The Comet is the most comfortable automobile you can buy.

B The Comet is the longest car in its price range.

C The price of the Comet is only $17,000.

D The Comet averages 22 miles per gallon of gasoline in city driving.

26   Josephina is reading a book called *City Under the Ocean*.

Which of these sentences is probably the last one in the story?

F The dome was finished, but now came the hard part, pumping the water out of the dome.

G The world said they couldn't do it, but they did, and the residents of Sea City celebrated their first anniversary with a huge party.

H "I have a suggestion you may find unbelievable," said Dr. Harrison, "but I have evidence it will work."

J While the dome was being built, the government was looking for families who would be willing to give up their current lives and settle the new city.

27 **Which of these sentences about weight lifting is <u>not</u> an opinion?**

A People who lift weights feel better than those who do not.

B The more weight you lift, the better you look.

C It is harder to lift weights than to swim or ski.

D Weight lifting burns up fewer calories than running the same amount of time.

STOP

Table of Contents
Language

Lesson 1   Punctuation

Examples   **Directions:** Mark the space for the punctuation mark that is needed in the sentence. Mark the space for "None" if no more punctuation marks are needed.

A   Are you coming with us

    A .   **B** !   **C** ?   **D** None

B   Helen's favorite subjects are math, science, and history.

    F ?   **G** "   **H** .   **J** None

Look carefully at all the answer choices before you choose the one you think is correct.

If a question is too difficult, skip it and come back to it later.

Practice

1   "The race starts at seven o'clock, answered Scottie.

    A ?   **B** "   **C** ,   **D** None

2   Be sure you turn the computer off before you come to bed

    F .   **G** ?   **H** !   **J** None

3   The television news reporter said "The election will be very close."

    A !   **B** .   **C** ,   **D** None

4   "When will you arrive in Florida?" asked Elaine

    F ,   **G** ?   **H** .   **J** None

5   The library is open every day except Sunday.

    A ,   **B** !   **C** ?   **D** None

6   Randy Cora and Alice took the bus from downtown to the stadium.

    F ,   **G** .   **H** ;   **J** None

GO ➤

For numbers 7-12, read each answer. Fill in the space for the choice that has a punctuation error. If there is no mistake, fill in the fourth answer space.

7   **A**   The beach is crowded
    B   It is a holiday, and
    C   many people are vacationing here.
    D   *(No mistakes)*

8   **F**   The school play is tomorrow.
    G   The three lead roles will be played
    H   by Shaneen Antonio and Beth.
    J   *(No mistakes)*

9   **A**   We couldnt find the car keys
    B   anywhere we looked. Then Mom
    C   remembered where they were.
    D   *(No mistakes)*

10   **F**
     G   45 Long Lane
     H   Barnes, CA 98204
     J   *(No mistakes)*   August 10, 1995

11   **A**   Dear Randy,
     B   How was your summer Mine went
     C   too quickly. School starts next week.
     D   *(No mistakes)*

12   **F**   I hope to see you at Thanksgiving.
     G   Your cousin
     H   Cecelia
     J   *(No mistakes)*

For numbers 13-15, read each sentence with a blank. Choose the word or words that fit best in the blank and show the correct punctuation.

13   Our town was founded by a group of settlers from Spain on _____ .

    A   Nov. 7 1750
    B   Nov 7, 1750
    C   Nov. 7, 1750
    D   Nov 7 1750

14   My _____ car is in the garage.

    F   sister
    G   sister's
    H   sisters'
    J   sisters

15   _____ you may to the movies, but be home by ten o'clock.

    A   Yes
    B   Yes;
    C   "Yes"
    D   Yes,

Choose the correct answer for number 16.

16   What is the correct way to begin a friendly letter?

    F   Dear Alice:
    G   Dear Alice
    H   Dear Alice,
    J   Dear Alice.

STOP

ANSWER ROWS   7 Ⓐ Ⓑ Ⓒ Ⓓ   9 Ⓐ Ⓑ Ⓒ Ⓓ   11 Ⓐ Ⓑ Ⓒ Ⓓ   13 Ⓐ Ⓑ Ⓒ Ⓓ   15 Ⓐ Ⓑ Ⓒ Ⓓ
               8 Ⓕ Ⓖ Ⓗ Ⓙ   10 Ⓕ Ⓖ Ⓗ Ⓙ   12 Ⓕ Ⓖ Ⓗ Ⓙ   14 Ⓕ Ⓖ Ⓗ Ⓙ   16 Ⓕ Ⓖ Ⓗ Ⓙ

Examples   **Directions:** Mark the space for the answer that shows correct punctuation and capitalization. Mark the space for "Correct as it is" if the underlined part is correct.

A   A Yes you may go to the labor day picnic.

    B On saturday we will celebrate my mother's Birthday.

    C The name of the book is *Holiday Origins*.

    D What is your favorite holiday.

B   Which of these tennis rackets is <u>yours</u>?

    F your's?

    G yours.

    H your's.

    J Correct as it is

Remember, you are looking for the answer that shows correct capitalization and punctuation.

If you are not sure which answer is correct, take your best guess.

Practice

1   A No, Robert is not here right now.

    B Yes the rest of the group is ready to go to the hotel.

    C No, the Hotel is not the same one we stayed in last year

    D Yes we will wait for robert?

2   F It rained, after we washed, the windows.

    G In the kitchen, we had to sweep the floor wash it and then wax it.

    H The worst job is moving the Furniture so we can vacuum.

    J The children helped clean the living room, dining room, and kitchen.

3   A The school band toured seven cities throughout the united states.

    B The city that was the most surprising was Detroit, Michigan.

    C In Gary Indiana we had the largest crowd.

    D We rode a bus from Trenton, New, Jersey all the way to Chicago, Illinois.

4   My shoes are <u>new but</u> they are already dirty from the hike.

    F new but,

    G new. But

    H new, but

    J Correct as it is

5   The manager <u>announced, "All</u> items marked with a red tag are half price."

    A announced, "all

    B announced "All

    C announced. "All

    D Correct as it is

6   <u>Seattle Washington</u> has great restaurants.

    F Seattle Washington,

    G Seattle, Washington

    H Seattle, Washington.

    J Correct as it is

GO

(7) The <u>pacific ocean</u> is a huge body of water. It extends from

(8) Alaska all the way to Antarctica and is many <u>thousand's of miles</u> wide. Because of its size, areas of the great ocean have many

(9) different climate <u>patterns.</u> In the far north and far south, it is very

(10) cold. In the middle, however, the Pacific warms places <u>like hawaii</u> Fiji, and Guam.

7
A Pacific ocean
B Pacific Ocean
C Pacific ocean,
D Correct as it is

8
F thousands of miles
G thousands' of miles
H thousands, of miles
J Correct as it is

9
A patterns?
B patterns'.
C pattern's.
D Correct as it is

10
F like, Hawaii
G like Hawaii,
H like, hawaii,
J Correct as it is

(11)   Jan. 14 1995

Upstate Road Racers

17 Main St.

Albany, NY 12201

(12) <u>dear mr. Dougherty</u>

Please send me a registration form for the upcoming race. My

(13) <u>friends and I</u> want to enter our team.

(14)   Sincerely yours

Vince Arno

11
A Jan. 14, 1995,
B Jan, 14, 1995
C Jan. 14, 1995
D Correct as it is

12
F Dear Mr. Dougherty:
G Dear Mr. dougherty:
H Dear mr. dougherty,
J Correct as it is

13
A friends, and I
B friends, and I,
C friends. And I
D Correct as it is

14
F sincerely yours
G Sincerely yours,
H Sincerely yours:
J Correct as it is

GO

ANSWER ROWS
7 Ⓐ Ⓑ Ⓒ Ⓓ   9 Ⓐ Ⓑ Ⓒ Ⓓ   11 Ⓐ Ⓑ Ⓒ Ⓓ   13 Ⓐ Ⓑ Ⓒ Ⓓ
8 Ⓕ Ⓖ Ⓗ Ⓙ   10 Ⓕ Ⓖ Ⓗ Ⓙ   12 Ⓕ Ⓖ Ⓗ Ⓙ   14 Ⓕ Ⓖ Ⓗ Ⓙ

62

For numbers 15 and 16, read the sentence with a blank. Mark the space beside the answer choice that fits best in the blank and has correct capitalization and punctuation.

15 The house we live in was finished on _____

    A november 20, 1990.
    B november 20, 1990,
    C November 20 1990?
    D November 20, 1990.

16 _____ kind of fish do you like?" asked the clerk.

    F "What
    G What
    H "what
    J "What,

Jim wrote this report about careers in health care. Read the report and use it to do numbers 17-20.

> When young people talk about a career in health
> **(1)**
> care, they usually think of Doctors and Nurses.
>
> What they don't realize is that there are many more
> **(2)**
> opportunities available? These other opportunities
>   **(3)**
> include things like physical therapist occupational
>
> therapist, and lab technician. Many experts believe
>   **(4)**
> the need for these positions is growing faster than
>
> most other careers.

17 In sentence 1, Doctors and Nurses is best written —

    A doctors and nurses
    B doctors, and nurses
    C Doctors and nurses
    D As it is

18 In sentence 2, available? is best written —

    F available!
    G available,
    H available.
    J As it is

19 In sentence 3, physical therapist is best written —

    A physical, therapist,
    B physical therapist,
    C physical therapist;
    D As it is

20 In sentence 4, experts is best written —

    F expert's
    G experts'
    H experts,
    J As it is

Example

E1

Are you sure you remembered to pack the toothbrushes

  A .   **B** !   **C** ?   **D** None

---

1   Hand me the hammer Alvina.

  A ,   **B** ;   **C** ”   **D** None

2   Watch out for the ice in front of you!

  F ?   **G** .   **H** ,   **J** None

3   "This is the largest animal in the zoo, said the keeper.

  A .   **B** ,   **C** ”   **D** None

4   Put the milk eggs and butter in the refrigerator, please.

  F .   **G** ,   **H** ”   **J** None

For numbers 5-7, read each answer. Fill in the space for the choice that has a punctuation error. If there is no mistake, fill in the fourth answer space.

5   **A**   The computer store in the mall
       B   is having a sale on software
       C   from Wednesday, through Saturday.
       D   *(No mistakes)*

6   **F**   No, this is not the first time
       G   the dog has been on the bed. She
       H   does it almost every day.
       J   *(No mistakes)*

7   **A**   Denine had'nt been fishing
       B   for more than five minutes when
       C   she caught a huge bass.
       D   *(No mistakes)*

For numbers 8 and 9, read each sentence with a blank. Choose the word or words that fit best in the blank and show the correct punctuation.

8   "Read the book before you see the _____ suggested Brandon.

       F   movie,
       G   movie,"
       H   movie"
       J   movie."

9   How do you know when a watermelon is

       _____

       A   ripe.
       B   ripe?
       C   ripe'
       D   ripe!

GO

ANSWER ROWS   **E1** Ⓐ Ⓑ Ⓒ Ⓓ   **2** Ⓕ Ⓖ Ⓗ Ⓙ   **4** Ⓕ Ⓖ Ⓗ Ⓙ   **6** Ⓕ Ⓖ Ⓗ Ⓙ   **8** Ⓕ Ⓖ Ⓗ Ⓙ
                  1 Ⓐ Ⓑ Ⓒ Ⓓ   **3** Ⓐ Ⓑ Ⓒ Ⓓ   **5** Ⓐ Ⓑ Ⓒ Ⓓ   **7** Ⓐ Ⓑ Ⓒ Ⓓ   **9** Ⓐ Ⓑ Ⓒ Ⓓ

For numbers 10-13, read each group of sentences. Find the one that is written correctly and shows the correct capitalization and punctuation.

10 **F** Don't touch that wet paint!

   G what kind of paint did you buy for the kitchen.

   H The brushes are in a plastic bag in the Garage?

   J How long do you think it will take us to finish!

11 **A** Let's pack a lunch and go, to Midway lake, this afternoon.

   B Fishermen, swimmers, and boaters all use Midway Lake.

   C The Parking Area for the lake is large well-lighted and inexpensive.

   D We can rent a motorboat or sailboat when We get there.

12 **F** Lets stop at the Supermarket before we go home, suggested Andy.

   G Rita Ann "said, don't forget to buy paper towels."

   H "Do you have enough money to pay for all of this Henry inquired?"

   J "Where can we find salad dressing?" asked Norma.

13 **A** Our nation's capital is Washington, which is near Virginia.

   B The city of New York is on the atlantic ocean.

   C That dresser was made in Raleigh, North Carolina.

   D Which State is larger, California or Montana?

For numbers 14-17, read the sentence with a blank. Mark the space beside the answer choice that fits best in the blank and has correct capitalization and punctuation.

14 A lecture will be presented on Saturday by _____ .

   F Dr Nace
   G dr Nace
   H Dr. Nace
   J dr. Nace

15 _____ the coat you ordered arrived yesterday.

   A Yes,
   B yes
   C Yes
   D yes,

16 "Our train is on track _____ commented Harish.

   F Seven"
   G seven",
   H Seven,"
   J seven,"

17 When do you think we will be able to see _____

   A Mt Whitney.
   B Mt. Whitney?
   C Mt. Whitney.
   D mt. Whitney?

GO

For numbers 18-21, look at the underlined part of each sentence. Find the answer choice that shows the correct capitalization and punctuation for the underlined part.

18 "You will all have a chance to use the computer the teacher told the students.

   F computer"

   G computer,

   H computer,"

   J Correct as it is

20 You can go to the fair but your brother will have to go with you.

   F fair, but, your

   G fair, but your

   H fair but, your

   J Correct as it is

19 Apples, oranges, and bananas were in a bowl on the table.

   A apples, oranges,

   B Apples oranges

   C Apples oranges,

   D Correct as it is

21 Several bridges cross the Mississippi river in St. Louis.

   A Mississippi River

   B Mississippi River,

   C mississippi river

   D Correct as it is

For numbers 22-25, read the passage. Find the answer choice that shows the correct capitalization and punctuation for the underlined part.

For a class assignment, I decided to investigate where ten of

(22)   my friends' parents were born. I was surprised at what I found.

(23)   Even though we live in new Jersey, only four parents were born in

(24)   this state. The others were born in Pennsylvania New York and

Puerto Rico. For the next part of the assignment, I hope to find out

(25)   why this is true?

22 **F** friends parents
     G friend's parents
     H friends parent's
     J Correct as it is

23 **A** new jersey,
     B New Jersey,
     C New Jersey.
     D Correct as it is

24 **F** Pennsylvania, New York, and
     G Pennsylvania, New York and,
     H Pennsylvania, New York, and,
     J Correct as it is

25 **A** true!
     B True?
     C true.
     D Correct as it is

GO

Here is more of Jim's report about careers in health care. Read the report and use it to do numbers 26-29.

(1)
For many young people, becoming an emergency medical technician is an exciting possibility! An
(2)
EMT works in an ambulance an emergency helicopter, or an emergency room. The pay in this career is
(3)
good, and the personal rewards are tremendous.

(4)
Although their work can sometimes be sad, emergency medical technician's get a feeling of satisfaction from helping injured people. When I interviewed
(5)
John Sherman, an EMT who works in our area, he said, "When I'm finished and have helped save someone, it is the most wonderful feeling in the world." Mr. Sherman also said that there is a great
(6)
need for EMTs, and it is a career young people should consider.

26 In sentence 1, possibility! is best written —

F possibility?
G possibility
H possibility.
J As it is

27 In sentence 2, ambulance an is best written —

A ambulance. An
B ambulance, an
C ambulance; an
D As it is

28 In sentence 4, technician's is best written —

F technicians
G technicians'
H technicians's
J As it is

29 In sentence 5, said, "When is best written —

A said, "when
B said. "When
C said when
D As it is

67

ANSWER ROWS   **26** Ⓕ Ⓖ Ⓗ Ⓙ   **27** Ⓐ Ⓑ Ⓒ Ⓓ   **28** Ⓕ Ⓖ Ⓗ Ⓙ   **29** Ⓐ Ⓑ Ⓒ Ⓓ   NUMBER RIGHT _____

Lesson 4   Usage

Examples   **Directions:** Read the directions for each section. Fill in the circle for the answer you think is correct.

A _____ and Barbara will have to walk to school today.

  A Them

  B Her

  C Us

  D You

B **F** This morning I woke up early.

  G Tomorrow she went skiing.

  H Next year we moved to an apartment on Broad Street.

  J We will visit the science museum a few weeks ago.

If you are not sure which answer is correct, eliminate answers you know are wrong and then take your best guess.

Stay with your first answer choice. You should change an answer only if you are sure the one you marked is incorrect.

Practice

For numbers 1-3, choose the word or phrase that best completes the sentence.

1 _____ was the best movie I've ever seen.

  A That there

  B That

  C Them

  D Those

2 It is _____ today than yesterday.

  F cold

  G coldest

  H colder

  J more colder

3 Nicole _____ the science club soon.

  A will join

  B joined

  C join

  D joining

For numbers 4-6, choose the answer that is a complete and correctly written sentence.

4 **F** Art class once a week with students in another class.

  G Entering a painting in the show.

  H Drawing and painting enjoyed by many young people.

  J The pot you made is beautiful.

5 **A** The fire company responded quick to the call for help.

  B My family usually contributes to the fund drive for the fire company.

  C They were happily to see the ambulance.

  D Nicely people on the ambulance squad.

6 **F** You and me can finish this job.

  G It was too heavy for her and me to carry.

  H They agreed to give he and I some help.

  J I and Rachel will be able to do it.

GO

For numbers 7-12, read each answer choice. Fill in the space for the choice that has a usage error. If there is no mistake, fill in the fourth answer space.

7   A   If we had gotten to
    B   the lake earlier, we
    C   mighta caught more fish.
    D   *(No mistakes)*

8   F   There isn't no way
    G   we will be able to finish
    H   this project on time.
    J   *(No mistakes)*

9   A   Jamie called back.
    B   She said her mother will
    C   arriving about seven o'clock.
    D   *(No mistakes)*

10 F   Barry was not aware
    G   that we were planning
    H   a surprise party for him.
    J   *(No mistakes)*

11 A   We looked a long
    B   time before we finded
    C   the missing house keys.
    D   *(No mistakes)*

12 F   My cousin she is
    G   going to get her
    H   driver's license this year.
    J   *(No mistakes)*

For numbers 13 and 14, choose the best way to write the underlined part of each sentence. If the underlined part is correct, fill in the fourth answer space.

13 We were late for dinner **although** the traffic was heavy.

    A   because
    B   after
    C   so
    D   *(No change)*

14 The carpenter **finished** her work and put her tools away.

    F   finishing
    G   finish
    H   were finished
    J   *(No change)*

For numbers 15 and 16, choose the answer that is a complete and correctly written sentence.

15 A   Helping around the house with chores and cooking.
    B   If the trash basket is full to empty it into the can outside.
    C   Darren raked up the leaves and put them in a large bag.
    D   The vacuum cleaner heavy to carry up and down stairs.

16 F   We sat on the porch for an hour my uncle told us lots of stories.
    G   The funniest story was the one about the dog and the ball.
    H   My grandmother is over ninety years old we love to hear her family stories.
    J   Judy wrote an essay for school it was about her family history.

Here is more of Jim's report about careers in health care. Read the report and use it to do numbers 17—20.

Most health care careers <u>requiring</u> education
(1)
beyond high school. This education can last from
(2)
two to as many as ten years. People who commit
(3)
<u>theirselves</u> to a health care career are willing to

invest in this additional education.

The job market for health care professionals
(4)
varies from place to place. In rural areas, almost
(5)
every health care professional can find <u>an job</u>

because the demand is great. In large cities where
(6)
many people like to live, it is <u>hardly</u> to find a

job. It is usually true that finding a job in
(7)
health care is easier than in other professions. In
(8)
addition, the job market will be even better in the

future because the population is getting older.

17   In sentence 1, <u>requiring</u> is best written —

A   requires
B   required
C   require
D   As it is

18   In sentence 3, <u>theirselves</u> is best written —

F   themselves
G   ourselves
H   himself
J   As it is

19   In sentence 5, <u>an job</u> is best written —

A   a jobs
B   a job
C   an jobs
D   As it is

20   In sentence 6, <u>hardly</u> is best written —

F   more harder
G   harder
H   most hardest
J   As it is

STOP

Examples   Directions: Read the directions for each section. Fill in the circle for the answer you think is correct. For example A, choose the word that names the simple subject. For example B, choose the word that names the simple predicate. For example C, mark the answer choice that best combines the two sentences.

A Birds sometimes fly for thousands of miles.

    A   B   C   D

B A large brown dog jumped into the pond.

    F   G   H   J

C Dee Ann plays basketball.

    She plays well.

    A Dee Ann plays basketball and well.

    B Dee Ann plays basketball but well.

    C Dee Ann plays basketball well.

    D Dee Ann plays well basketball.

If you are not sure which answer choice is correct, say each one to yourself. The right answer usually sounds best.

Read the directions for each section and think about them when you choose the answer you think is correct.

Practice

For numbers 1-3, find the underlined part that is the simple subject of the sentence.

1 Two students won awards for their science projects.

      A   B   C   D

2 A beautiful stone wall divided the field into two parts.

      F   G H   J

3 Most of my friends enjoy pizza and sandwiches.

    A   B   C   D

For numbers 4-6, find the underlined part that is the simple predicate (verb) of the sentence.

4 The crowded bus stopped in front of the theater.

      F   G   H   J

5 A moose walked slowly from the woods into the lake.

    A   B   C   D

6 The trees on our block lost their leaves last week.

      F   G H   J

GO

For numbers 7-9, choose the answer that best combines the underlined sentences.

7 <u>Pedro finished his homework.</u>

<u>Pedro went to bed.</u>

   A Pedro finished his homework or went to bed.

   B Pedro finished his homework then went to bed.

   C Pedro finished his homework because he went to bed.

   D Going to bed, Pedro finished his homework.

8 <u>The truck brought the furniture to our house.</u>

<u>The truck was large.</u>

   F The large truck, which brought the furniture to our house.

   G The truck was large that brought the furniture to our house.

   H The truck brought the furniture to our house, and was large.

   J The large truck brought the furniture to our house.

9 <u>Arnie found a ball.</u>

<u>The ball was red.</u>

<u>He found it on the way to school.</u>

   A Finding a red ball, Arnie was on his way to school.

   B Arnie found a red ball on the way to school.

   C Arnie found a ball on the way to school that was red.

   D The red ball that Arnie found on the way to school.

For numbers 10 and 11, choose the best way of expressing the idea.

10 **F** The sidewalk is on Broad Street slippery.
     G On Broad Street is slippery the sidewalk.
     H The sidewalk on Broad Street is slippery.
     J The slippery sidewalk which is on Broad Street.

11 **A** The windows are dirty, but we should wash them.
     B The windows, they are dirty. We should wash them.
     C The windows are dirty. We should wash them.
     D We should wash the windows unless they are dirty.

Jim's report about health care continues here. Use the report to do numbers 12-15.

To succeed as a health care professional, you
(1)
need more than training. It is also important to
(2)
have good "people" skills. Knowing what to do and
(3)
how to communicate with patients.

In the United States today, health care is
(4)
changing. People are trying to keep the cost of
(5)
health care down. People are working harder to stay
(6)
healthy. Many politicians believe that one of our
(7)
national goals should be to make our health care

system the best in the world.

The changes in health care mean that changes
(8)
will be occurring now and in the future. Even so,
(9)
there will still be many jobs available.

12   Sentence 1 is best written —

F More than training to succeed as a
health care professional.
G As a health care professional, training is
more than you need.
H Training and more to succeed as a health
care professional.
J As it is

**13   Which sentence incorrectly repeats a
word or group of words?**

A 2
B 4
C 8
D 9

14   Which of these is *not* a sentence?

F 2
G 3
H 4
J 9

**15   How can sentences 5 and 6 best be
joined without changing their
meaning?**

A People trying to keep the cost of health
care down and staying healthy.
B Because they are healthy, people are
trying to keep the cost of health care
down.
C People are trying to keep the cost of
health care down, working harder, and
staying healthy.
D People are trying to keep the cost of
health care down and are working
harder to stay healthy.

Example   **Directions:** Read the directions for each section. Fill in the circle
for the answer you think is correct.

Read the paragraph below. Find the best topic sentence for the paragraph.

A _____ . Sailors must know a lot about both wind and water. In addition,
sailors must be able to respond quickly to change the sail or the tiller. When you see a
boat sail smoothly across a lake, you can be sure that someone is working very hard.

   A Motor boats and sail boats can be found on many bodies of water.

   B A sailboat is a graceful craft that gives you a great sense of freedom.

   C Millions of people enjoy water sports like sailing and fishing.

   D Sailing is a more complicated sport than it appears.

Be sure to look at all the answer choices before you choose the
one you think is correct.

Remember, a paragraph should focus on one idea. The correct
answer is the one that fits best with the rest of the paragraph.

Practice

Read the paragraph below. Find the best topic sentence for the paragraph.

1 _____ . In some cases, cities have built special parking facilities for bicyclists.
They have also added bicycle lanes to some city streets. The reason for this
encouragement is that commuting by bicycle cuts down on both traffic and air pollution.

   A Many cities are encouraging people to ride bicycles to work.

   B Bicycling is a sport that has grown in popularity in recent years.

   C Many cities are looking for ways to reduce the amount of traffic at rush hour.

   D A bicycle can be used for more than just recreation.

Find the answer choice that best develops the topic sentence below.

2   Our cat, Petunia, does the strangest thing.

   F We got her two years ago from a friend. Since then, Petunia has become an important
part of our family.

   G She is a gray cat with dark stripes. When I go to sleep at night, she loves to snuggle
up beside me.

   H For no reason at all, she just starts running around the house. Then, without
warning, Petunia finds a comfortable spot and falls sound asleep.

   J We also have a dog named Molly. Petunia and Molly get along well, and sometimes
they eat out of the same bowl.

For numbers 3 and 4, read the paragraph. Find the sentence that does not belong in the paragraph.

3   1. The National Weather Service is a part of the United States government.   2. Another part of the government is the National Park Service.   3. The National Weather Service is responsible for preparing weather maps and making forecasts.   4. Many businesses and individuals depend on the National Weather Service to plan their activities.

    A Sentence 1

    B Sentence 2

    C Sentence 3

    D Sentence 4

4   1. The water ouzel is a most remarkable bird.   2. Like many other birds, it feeds on insects.   3. Hummingbirds feed on nectar from flowers as well as insects.   4. But unlike other birds, the water ouzel often seeks its food by diving into a stream and walking along the bottom!

    F Sentence 1

    G Sentence 2

    H Sentence 3

    J Sentence 4

For numbers 5 and 6, read the paragraph. Find the sentence that best fits the blank in the paragraph.

5   Rashad decided to join the ski club at his school. _____ . Once a week, the ski club takes a bus to a ski area about two hours from school. There they are able to rent skis and buy a lift ticket for half-price.

    A There were twelve other clubs at his school.

    B He was a good student and enjoyed doing different things.

    C His older sister had been in the history club at the same school.

    D He had never skied before, but thought it looked like fun.

6   During the nineteenth century, canals were an important means of transporting goods from place to place in America. One of the most important was the Erie Canal. _____. The Erie Canal allowed goods to be exchanged between the Midwest and the large cities of the East.

    F It went from Lake Erie to the Hudson River.

    G Lake Erie is one of the Great Lakes.

    H Canals were also important in other parts of the world, especially Europe.

    J The barges that were loaded with goods were pulled by mules.

GO

For numbers 7-9, use the paragraph below to answer the questions.

> [1]One of Lucy's friends, Harold, invited her to a special gym. [2]This gym has practice walls and safety equipment. [3]Lucy enjoys many sports, especially skiing and hiking. [4]Harold taught Lucy how to climb safely at the gym. [5]When he was sure Lucy was confident, he brought her to Irwin Cliff. [6]There Lucy made her first climb. [7]Harold is an experienced climber who works as a teacher at the gym.

7 Choose the best first sentence for this paragraph.

A I have an older sister named Lucy.
B My sister Lucy is one of my best friends.
C My sister Lucy recently tried a new sport, rock climbing.
D Rock climbing is a sport that is becoming more popular.

8 Which sentence should be left out of this paragraph?

F Sentence 1
G Sentence 3
H Sentence 4
J Sentence 5

9 Where is the best place for sentence 7?

A Between sentences 1 and 2
B Between sentences 3 and 4
C Before sentence 1
D Where it is now

10 Which of the following would be most appropriate in a letter asking for information about renting a houseboat on a lake?

F My sister, my parents, and I are interested in visiting Lake Patterson. Can you send me information about how the lake was created and what kind of fish are in the lake? Are there stores around the lake where we can buy things?

G Last year, some of my friends visited Lake Patterson. This year, my family would like to do the same thing. Can you send me information on how to get to the lake and what to do when we get there? Is it crowded on weekends? What kinds of boats can we rent when we get there?

H My family recently moved here from Minnesota. There are many lakes in Minnesota. We heard that there are many fun things to do at Lake Patterson. Can you please send us information about the lake? What is the weather like in the fall? Do you need a fishing license to fish there?

J My family is thinking about renting a houseboat on Lake Patterson. Please send me any brochures you have telling how much it will cost and what we should bring. I would also be interested in reading any other information you have on renting a houseboat on the lake.

GO

Here is more of Jim's report about health care careers. Use the report to do numbers 11-14.

A career in health care has many benefits. One
(1)   (2)
benefit. is the feeling of helping others. This
                                       (3)
might sound a little corny, but all of the people I

interviewed agreed that this was an important part

of their career. Some workers don't help anyone.
                          (4)
Another benefit is good working conditions. The
(5)   (6)
work is hard and the hours are long, but most

people said they enjoyed working where they did.

They also said they felt secure that their jobs
(7)
would be around for years to come.

The biggest problem people mentioned was stress.
(8)
Workers in the health care field have to respond to

emergencies almost every day. In addition, they
                                       (9)
spend a lot of time with sick or injured people who

don't get better.

11 Which sentence could be added before sentence 6?

A Hospitals are usually clean and comfortable.
B Major cities often have one or more large hospitals.
C This is something other workers don't have.
D Poor working conditions make workers unhappy.

12 What is the topic sentence of the first paragraph?

F 1
G 2
H 3
J 4

13 Which of these could be added after sentence 9?

A Some people spend many months in a hospital.
B This makes workers sad.
C Being in a hurry often makes people feel they are stressed.
D In an emergency room, there is a lot of stress.

14 Which sentence does *not* belong in the story?

F 1
G 3
H 4
J 7

Example   Directions: Find the underlined part that is the simple predicate (verb) of the sentence.

E1

The <u>moon</u> <u>seems</u> <u>larger</u> than <u>usual</u> tonight.

    A   B   C   D

For number 1, choose the word or phrase that best completes the sentence.

1   My hair _____ slowly because it is so long.

   A to dry

   B drying

   C dry

   D dries

For number 2, choose the answer that is a complete and correctly written sentence.

2   **F** The rain fell hard today than it did last week.

   G The moon is brightest tonight than it will be next week.

   H The longest day of the year is usually the twenty-first of June.

   J It was too darker for us to see the owl in the tree.

For numbers 3-5, read each answer choice. Fill in the space for the choice that has a usage error. If there is no mistake, fill in the fourth answer space.

3   **A**   The cat scratched the
      B table when she jumped
      C up on it last night.
      D *(No mistakes)*

4   **F**   The three foolish hikers
      G knowed it was dangerous
      H but started the climb anyway.
      J *(No mistakes)*

5   **A**   We wanted to order
      B the chicken salad, but
      C Ina she said it wasn't very good.
      D *(No mistakes)*

For number 6, find the underlined part that is the simple subject of the sentence.

6   <u>Bread</u> <u>rises</u> because of the <u>yeast</u> in the <u>batter</u>.
     F **G**   **H**   **J**

For number 7, find the underlined part that is the simple predicate (verb) of the sentence.

7   The <u>door</u> to the <u>kitchen</u> <u>blew</u> open <u>because</u> of the wind.
     A   **B** **C**   **D**

          GO ▷

ANSWER ROWS **E1** Ⓐ Ⓑ Ⓒ Ⓓ   **2** Ⓕ Ⓖ Ⓗ Ⓙ   **4** Ⓕ Ⓖ Ⓗ Ⓙ   **6** Ⓕ Ⓖ Ⓗ Ⓙ
               1 Ⓐ Ⓑ Ⓒ Ⓓ   **3** Ⓐ Ⓑ Ⓒ Ⓓ   **5** Ⓐ Ⓑ Ⓒ Ⓓ   **7** Ⓐ Ⓑ Ⓒ Ⓓ

For numbers 8-10, choose the answer that best combines the underlined sentences.

8 Anzia went to the store.

Victor went to the store.

F Anzia went to the store and Victor went to the store.

G Anzia went to the store and Victor.

H Anzia and Victor went to the store.

J Anzia went and Victor went to the store.

9 The parade started at ten o'clock.

The parade started in the town square.

A The parade started at ten o'clock in the town square.

B At ten o'clock the parade started and in the town square.

C The parade, which started at ten o'clock in the town square.

D The parade started at ten o'clock and in the town square.

10 Roddy painted the garage.

The paint was bright.

The paint was red.

F Roddy painted the garage with paint that was bright and paint that was red.

G Roddy painted the garage with bright red paint.

H Roddy painted the garage with red paint.

J Roddy painted the garage with paint that was red and bright.

For numbers 11 and 12, choose the best way of expressing the idea.

11 **A** The newspaper arrives about seven o'clock in the morning.
B The newspaper about seven o'clock arrives in the morning.
C About seven o'clock in the morning arrives the newspaper.
D In the morning arrives the newspaper about seven o'clock.

12 **F** The rain came in and Lynette left the bedroom window open.
G The open bedroom window left by Lynette and the rain came in.
H Lynette left open the bedroom window because the rain came in.
J Lynette left the bedroom window open and the rain came in.

GO

Read the paragraph below. Find the best topic sentence for the paragraph.

13 _____ . By pressing just a few buttons, you can speak with someone almost anywhere in the world. If you connect a computer to a telephone, you can gain access to almost unlimited information contained in other computers. It is not an exaggeration to say the telephone is a modern miracle.

    A The telephone is one of the simplest household devices to use.

    B Telephones can be found in almost every home in America.

    C A telephone is a truly remarkable device.

    D The telephone was invented more than a hundred years ago.

Find the answer choice that best develops the topic sentence.

14 The world was a very different place a hundred million years ago.

    F North America and Europe were still one continent. The Rocky Mountains had not yet formed, and dinosaurs were the dominant life form.

    G Scientists are not sure why dinosaurs disappeared. They think this happened about sixty-five million years ago.

    H Even today, the world is changing. Volcanoes and earthquakes are slowly changing the face of the planet.

    J Wind, rain, and other natural forces are constantly changing the surface of the earth. Animals like dinosaurs became extinct.

Read the paragraph below. Find the sentence that does not belong in the paragraph.

15 1. The Anderson family follows an interesting tradition each January first. 2. Everyone sits around the living room floor and looks at old family photos. 3. The older family members tell stories about the people in the pictures. 4. Many young people are not familiar with their ancestors.

    A Sentence 1

    B Sentence 2

    C Sentence 3

    D Sentence 4

Read the paragraph below. Find the sentence that best fits the blank in the paragraph.

16 An almanac is a wonderful resource for finding information. _____. A good almanac will contain everything from ancient history to colorful maps. Some almanacs also list the important events from the year they were published.

    F Another popular resource is an encyclopedia.

    G It is a collection of information on many topics.

    H Some people prefer to use computers to do their research.

    J You still must know what information you are looking for.

GO >

Below is the conclusion of Jim's report about health care careers. Read the report and use it to do numbers 17-20.

To end my report, I would like to talk about how
(1)
you make a career in health care. The first thing
(2)
to do is stay in school. Almost every job in health
(3)
care requires at least a high school diploma.

Next, how much additional time you want to spend
(4)
in school. If you want to go to college for two to
(5)
four years, you can become a nurse, therapist,

emergency medical technician, or lab technician. If
(6)
you want to become a doctor, you will have to go to

college for at least eight years.

Finally, you <u>have shown</u> that you are
(7)
trustworthy, dependable, and capable. An easy way
(8)
to do this is to volunteer in a hospital while you

are still in school. Volunteering shows you are
(9)
willing to work and helps you get letters of

reference from the people you work with.

17 How is sentence 2 best written?

A The first thing in school is to stay.
B Staying in school, and the first thing.
C In school to stay is the first thing.
D As it is

18 Which sentence could be added after sentence 3?

F Many young people drop out of school before they get a diploma.
G This includes jobs like maintenance worker, cook, or aide.
H Some people don't want to go to college.
J This is also true in other careers.

19 Which group of words is not a complete thought?

A 2
B 4
C 7
D 9

20 In sentence 7, <u>have shown</u> is best written —

F will have shown
G was showing
H have to show
J As it is

81

UNIT 3   SPELLING

Lesson 8   Spelling Skills

Examples   **Directions:** Follow the directions for each section. Choose the answer you think is correct.

Find the word that is spelled correctly and fits best in the blank.	Choose the phrase in which the underlined word is <u>not</u> spelled correctly.
A We parked in the _____ part of town. A centrul B centeral C central D centrle	B F <u>noisey</u> room G tall <u>building</u> H easy <u>problem</u> J <u>spend</u> money

Read the directions carefully. Be sure you know if you should look for the correctly spelled word or the incorrectly spelled word.

If you know which answer is correct, mark it and move on to the next item.

Practice

For numbers 1-5, find the word that is spelled correctly and fits best in the blank.

1   We can _____ the gymnasium.

    A   decarate
    B   decorait
    C   decorrate
    D   decorate

2   Gina wrote me a _____ .

    F   leter
    G   lettre
    H   letterr
    J   letter

3   Being _____ is always a good idea.

    A   palite
    B   polite
    C   polight
    D   pollite

4   It took us hours to _____ the puzzle.

    F   solv
    G   salve
    H   solve
    J   soulve

5   Our cat has long _____ .

    A   whiskers
    B   wiskers
    C   whiskurs
    D   wiskres

For numbers 6-8, read the phrases. Choose the phrase in which the underlined word is <u>not</u> spelled correctly.

6   F   healthy <u>plant</u>
    G   <u>hungry</u> birds
    H   wonderful <u>gift</u>
    J   <u>accurrate</u> answer

7   A   <u>enought</u> room
    B   wet <u>paint</u>
    C   <u>loud</u> noise
    D   seem <u>foolish</u>

8   F   <u>funny</u> story
    G   beautiful <u>island</u>
    H   <u>grow</u> quickly
    J   speed <u>limit</u>

GO

For numbers 9-11, read each answer. Fill in the space for the choice that has a spelling error. If there is no mistake, fill in the last answer space.

9 A lazy
   B offer
   C replace
   D victory
   E (No mistakes)

10 F poorly
   G surfice
   H mislead
   J trust
   K (No mistakes)

11 A pionear
   B servant
   C nervous
   D welcome
   E (No mistakes)

For numbers 12-14, read each phrase. One of the underlined words is not spelled correctly for the way it is used in the phrase. Fill in the space for the word that is not spelled correctly.

12 F vanish quickly
   G call twice
   H chews friends
   J work quietly

13 A large pile
   B loud laugh
   C needed help
   D least a car

14 F deep harbor
   G died cloth
   H pair of pants
   J knowing an answer

For numbers 15-18, find the underlined part that is misspelled. If all the words are spelled correctly, mark the space under No mistake.

15 Kari's family remained in northern Utah for only a brief time. No mistake.
                  A   B   C   D

16 This map will gide you to the national forest campground. No mistake.
                  F   G   H   J

17 A madgor highway in our area was closed because of an accident. No mistake.
      A   B   C   D

18 Will anyone be home to recieve the package when it arrives? No mistake.
         F   G   H   J

Examples   Directions: For E1, find the word that is spelled correctly and fits best in the blank. For E2, choose the phrase in which the underlined word is <u>not</u> spelled correctly.

E1

This coat is not _____ the price.

A   wirth
B   werth
C   wurth
D   worth

E2

F   <u>enormous</u> sandwich
G   bright <u>color</u>
H   <u>bukle</u> a belt
J   run <u>quickly</u>

For numbers 1-6, find the word that is spelled correctly and fits best in the blank.

1   I will finish this in a _____ .

A   momint
B   moamint
C   moment
D   moement

2   A loud noise _____ the birds.

F   scared
G   scaird
H   scard
J   scareded

3   The store is in a good _____ .

A   locashun
B   locashin
C   locatin
D   location

4   Kim is a _____ visitor at the gym.

F   regulur
G   regular
H   reguler
J   regalar

5   The students were _____ for their bravery.

A   honered
B   honord
C   honard
D   honored

6   A _____ writer visited our school.

F   famous
G   famus
H   fameous
J   fameus

For numbers 7-10, read the phrase. Choose the phrase in which the underlined word is not spelled correctly.

7   A   <u>caught</u> fish

B   <u>loosen</u> a knot

C   good <u>skech</u>

D   famous <u>author</u>

8   F   fishing <u>lodge</u>

G   <u>aproach</u> slowly

H   book <u>cover</u>

J   <u>recent</u> news

9   A   <u>learn</u> quickly

B   strong <u>oder</u>

C   gain <u>freedom</u>

D   <u>gather</u> shells

10   F   <u>exack</u> change

G   unknown <u>cause</u>

H   will <u>forgive</u>

J   <u>harmless</u> snake

GO ▷

For numbers 11-13, read each answer. Fill in the space for the choice that has a spelling error. If there is no mistake, fill in the last answer space.

For numbers 14-16, read each phrase. One of the underlined words is not spelled correctly for the way it is used in the phrase. Fill in the space for the word that is not spelled correctly.

11 A numb
    B ignore
    C worn
    D purchace
    E (No mistakes)

14 F last night
    G do a favor
    H road in a car
    J hair brush

12 F story
    G praise
    H inform
    J famous
    K (No mistakes)

15 A seem unfair
    B draw pictures
    C fishing real
    D stay home

13 A machene
    B silence
    C oppose
    D modern
    E (No mistakes)

16 F maid by hand
    G funny poem
    H arrive late
    J rough weather

For numbers 17-20, find the underlined part that is misspelled. If all the words are spelled correctly, mark the space under No mistake.

17 The stew we had for dinner had an unusual flaver. No mistake.
        A   B   C   D

18 The desert begins just a few miles beyond the mountains. No mistake.
        F   G   H   J

19 The kitchen in this apartment is simpley too small. No mistake.
        A   B   C   D

20 Lyman's parints invited us to a picnic at their house. No mistake.
            F   G   H   J

STOP

Lesson 10   Study Skills

Example   **Directions:** Follow the directions for each section. Choose the answer you think is correct.

Table of Contents

Chapter	Page
1 The History of Boats	1
2 Sailboats	21
3 Motor Boats	35
4 Boating Safety	42

A Which chapter probably tells about the types of fuels used in boats.

A Chapter 1
B Chapter 2
C Chapter 3
D Chapter 4

Before you mark your answer, compare it to any reference source that is part of the question.

It may help if you read difficult questions twice.

Practice

The illustration below shows a set of encyclopedias. Each of the numbered volumes holds information about topics that begin with the letters shown on that volume. Use the picture to do numbers 1-2.

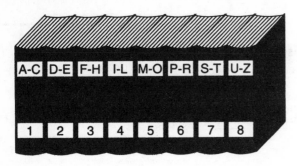

1 Which of these topics would be found in Volume 7?

A the life of Stephen Douglas
B how to climb tall mountains
C typical weather in different cities
D why stars twinkle

2 In which volume would you find information about shirts, pants, coats, and other clothing you wear?

F Volume 1   H Volume 6
G Volume 3   J Volume 8

Read each question below. Mark the space for the answer you think is correct.

3 Look at these guide words from a dictionary page.

easel–echo

Which word could be found on the page?

A ear   C ebb
B essay   D end

4 Look at these guide words from a dictionary page.

troop–trust

Which word could be found on the page?

F tusk   H trombone
G trunk   J try

5 Which of these is a main heading that includes the other three words?

A School
B Building
C Bank
D Store

GO

ANSWER ROWS   A ⒶⒷⒸⒹ   1 ⒶⒷⒸⒹ   2 ⒻⒼⒽⒿ   3 ⒶⒷⒸⒹ   4 ⒻⒼⒽⒿ   5 ⒶⒷⒸⒹ

As part of a class project on travel, Bonnie asked 100 people at a mall which of eight states they had visited. The graph below shows the results of her interviews. Study the graph, then do numbers 6-9.

STATES VISITED

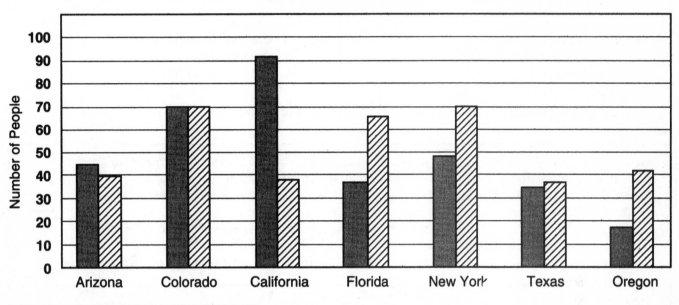

6 Which state was visited by the most women?

F   New York
G   California
H   Colorado
J   Oregon

7 How many men visited Arizona?

A   40
B   45
C   70
D   38

8 Which state was visited by more than twice as many men as women?

F   California
G   Texas
H   Colorado
J   Oregon

9 Based on the graph, which of these statements is true?

A   More women visited Texas than Arizona.
B   Men like New York more than women do.
C   The same number of women and men visited Colorado.
D   Women travel more often than men.

Lesson 11 Test Yourself

Examples Directions: Read each question. Mark the answer you think is correct.

E1

Where would you look to find the population of the major American cities?

A in a newspaper
B in an atlas
C in a magazine
D in a dictionary

E2

In which part of a book would you find definitions of terms in the book?

F the index
G the table of contents
H the glossary
J the bibliography

Use the sample dictionary entries and the Pronunciation Guide below to answer numbers 1-4.

rate [rāt] *n.* 1. the amount of payment associated with a calculation: *a high rate of bank interest* 2. a quantity or amount of something: *a speed rate of 40 miles per hour* 3. a fixed charge or price per unit: *a rate of $1.00 a pound* 4. a statement of quality: *first rate school* *v.* 5. to arrange in order of quality: *to rate the entries in a contest*
rat•i•fy [rat′ ə fī] *v.* 1. to confirm by expressing consent or approval 2. to validate: *The Congress will ratify the amendment.*
ra•tion [rash′ ən] *n.* 1. a fixed amount *v.* 2. to limit the amount or use of: *to ration food*

Pronunciation Guide:
act, wāy, dâre, ärt, set, ēqual, big, ĭce, box, ōver, hôrse, bo͝ok, to͞ol, us, cūte, tûrn; ə= a in *alone*, e in *mitten*, o in *actor*, u in *circus*

1 The "a" in *rate* sounds most like the vowel sound in the word—

A way
B act
C art
D turn

2 Which definition best fits the word *rate* as it is used in the sentence below?

The judges were asked to rate the quality of seven different restaurants.

F 2
G 3
H 4
J 5

3 What is the correct way to divide *ratify* into syllables?

A rati-fy
B rat-if-y
C ra-tif-y
D rat-i-fy

4 In which of these sentences is *ration* used as a verb?

F The ration of water was not enough during the hottest days.
G Each person was given a ration of food for the trip.
H The hikers will ration their food to be sure they have enough.
J You will be thirsty later if you drink your ration of water too soon.

Leroy, Shana, and Darcy are doing a project about businesses in their town. Keep this topic in mind when you do numbers 5-8.

5 Before they begin the project, the three students want to get an idea of the different businesses that operate in their town. They should look in—

A an atlas
B an encyclopedia under "business"
C the dictionary under "business"
D the Yellow Pages of the telephone book

6 Which of these should not be included in the project?

F the kinds of businesses in town
G what business owners get paid
H how businesses got started
J where businesses are located

7 Darcy found a book in the library about the history of the town. Where should she look to see if it has a chapter about the early businesses in the town?

A the table of contents
B the index
C the bibliography
D the glossary

8 Shana made a web to help her interview business owners. Which of these belongs in the web?

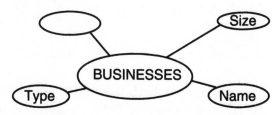

F idea
G location
H neighbors
J parking

Study this table of contents from a book about television. Then do numbers 9 and 10.

Table of Contents

Chapter		Page
1	The Invention of Television	1
2	The Earliest Years	19
3	TV Becomes Popular	37
4	Live Television	51
5	Famous TV Shows	65
6	Daytime TV	79
7	Evening TV	90
8	Famous TV Stars	117
9	Educational TV	136
10	Cable TV	152
11	Satellite TV	178
12	The Future of Television	202

9 When the idea of television was first discussed, several different people tried to build televisions. In which chapter might you read about them?

A Chapter 1
B Chapter 3
C Chapter 8
D Chapter 12

10 Which of these sentences might you find in Chapter 3?

F Television reception is improving each year because of advances in technology.
G There are important differences between television shows that appear during the day and at night.
H During the 1950s, television shows were shown "live," which means people at home saw the action as it happened.
J It wasn't until after 1950 that televisions began to appear in many American homes.

GO

Use this card from a library card catalog to do numbers 11-14.

922.64

C   **Cohen, Scott**
       Mountain Biking across America / Scott
       Cohen; photographs by Andrea Chavez.
       Maps by Millie Lindall.
       Chicago: Fat Tire Press, 1993.
       240 p.; photos and maps; 23 cm
       (The Adventure series, volume 2)

       1. Biking   2. Travel   3. Adventure
       4. America   I. Title

11 What is the title of this book?

A *Fat Tires*
B *Biking and Travel*
C *Mountain Biking across America*
D *The Adventure Series*

12 According to the card, other books on the same subject can be found in the card catalog under which of these headings?

F Cohen
G Author
H Across
J Travel

13 What type of library catalog card is this?

A Title
B Subject
C Publisher
D Author

14 Which of these would help you locate the book in the library?

F 922.64
G 1993
H 240 p.
J 23 cm

A group of students is taking a nature walk. They made this outline to help them identify different things on their walk. Study the outline, then do numbers 15-17.

Nature Walk

I. _____
    A. Leaves
    B. Flowers
    C. Fruit
II. Birds
    A. Color
    B. Size
    C. _____
    D. Habitat
    E. Food
III. Rocks
    A. Color
    B. Size
    C. Texture
    D. Location

15 Line I of the outline is blank. Which of these fits best there?

A Hiking
B Plants
C Oceans
D Roots

16 Line II-C of the outline is blank. Which of these fits best there?

F Name
G Flying
H Robin
J Song

17 Suppose the students wanted to add a fourth major heading to the outline. Which of these would make the most sense?

A Animals
B Feathers
C Rivers
D Pets

STOP

90

ANSWER ROWS **11** Ⓐ Ⓑ Ⓒ Ⓓ   **13** Ⓐ Ⓑ Ⓒ Ⓓ   **15** Ⓐ Ⓑ Ⓒ Ⓓ   **17** Ⓐ Ⓑ Ⓒ Ⓓ
             12 Ⓕ Ⓖ Ⓗ Ⓙ   **14** Ⓕ Ⓖ Ⓗ Ⓙ   **16** Ⓕ Ⓖ Ⓗ Ⓙ   NUMBER RIGHT _____

To the Student:

These tests will give you a chance to put the tips you have learned to work.

A few last reminders...

- Be sure you understand all the directions before you begin each test. You may ask the teacher questions about the directions if you do not understand them.
- Work as quickly as you can during each test.
- When you change an answer, be sure to erase your first mark completely.

- You can guess at an answer or skip difficult items and go back to them later.
- Use the tips you have learned whenever you can.
- It is OK to be a little nervous. You may even do better.

Now that you have completed the lessons in this unit, you are on your way to scoring high!

STUDENT'S NAME			SCHOOL
LAST	FIRST	MI	TEACHER

FEMALE ○   MALE ○

BIRTHDATE

MONTH	DAY	YEAR
JAN ○	⓪ ⓪	⓪
FEB ○	① ①	①
MAR ○	② ②	②
APR ○	③ ③	③
MAY ○	④	④
JUN ○	⑤	⑤ ⑤
JUL ○	⑥	⑥ ⑥
AUG ○	⑦	⑦ ⑦
SEP ○	⑧	⑧ ⑧
OCT ○	⑨	⑨ ⑨
NOV ○		
DEC ○		

GRADE

③ ④ ⑤

(Name grid columns with bubbles A–Z)

PART 1   LANGUAGE MECHANICS

E1 Ⓐ Ⓑ Ⓒ Ⓓ	4 Ⓕ Ⓖ Ⓗ Ⓙ	8 Ⓕ Ⓖ Ⓗ Ⓙ	12 Ⓕ Ⓖ Ⓗ Ⓙ	16 Ⓕ Ⓖ Ⓗ Ⓙ	19 Ⓐ Ⓑ Ⓒ Ⓓ
1 Ⓐ Ⓑ Ⓒ Ⓓ	5 Ⓐ Ⓑ Ⓒ Ⓓ	9 Ⓐ Ⓑ Ⓒ Ⓓ	13 Ⓐ Ⓑ Ⓒ Ⓓ	17 Ⓐ Ⓑ Ⓒ Ⓓ	20 Ⓕ Ⓖ Ⓗ Ⓙ
2 Ⓕ Ⓖ Ⓗ Ⓙ	6 Ⓕ Ⓖ Ⓗ Ⓙ	10 Ⓕ Ⓖ Ⓗ Ⓙ	14 Ⓕ Ⓖ Ⓗ Ⓙ	18 Ⓕ Ⓖ Ⓗ Ⓙ	21 Ⓐ Ⓑ Ⓒ Ⓓ
3 Ⓐ Ⓑ Ⓒ Ⓓ	7 Ⓐ Ⓑ Ⓒ Ⓓ	11 Ⓐ Ⓑ Ⓒ Ⓓ	15 Ⓐ Ⓑ Ⓒ Ⓓ		

PART 2   LANGUAGE EXPRESSION

E1 Ⓐ Ⓑ Ⓒ Ⓓ	4 Ⓕ Ⓖ Ⓗ Ⓙ	8 Ⓕ Ⓖ Ⓗ Ⓙ	12 Ⓕ Ⓖ Ⓗ Ⓙ	15 Ⓐ Ⓑ Ⓒ Ⓓ	18 Ⓕ Ⓖ Ⓗ Ⓙ
1 Ⓐ Ⓑ Ⓒ Ⓓ	5 Ⓐ Ⓑ Ⓒ Ⓓ	9 Ⓐ Ⓑ Ⓒ Ⓓ	13 Ⓐ Ⓑ Ⓒ Ⓓ	16 Ⓕ Ⓖ Ⓗ Ⓙ	19 Ⓐ Ⓑ Ⓒ Ⓓ
2 Ⓕ Ⓖ Ⓗ Ⓙ	6 Ⓕ Ⓖ Ⓗ Ⓙ	10 Ⓕ Ⓖ Ⓗ Ⓙ	14 Ⓕ Ⓖ Ⓗ Ⓙ	17 Ⓐ Ⓑ Ⓒ Ⓓ	20 Ⓕ Ⓖ Ⓗ Ⓙ
3 Ⓐ Ⓑ Ⓒ Ⓓ	7 Ⓐ Ⓑ Ⓒ Ⓓ	11 Ⓐ Ⓑ Ⓒ Ⓓ			

PART 3   SPELLING

E1 Ⓐ Ⓑ Ⓒ Ⓓ	3 Ⓐ Ⓑ Ⓒ Ⓓ	7 Ⓐ Ⓑ Ⓒ Ⓓ	11 Ⓐ Ⓑ Ⓒ Ⓓ Ⓔ	15 Ⓐ Ⓑ Ⓒ Ⓓ	19 Ⓐ Ⓑ Ⓒ Ⓓ
E2 Ⓕ Ⓖ Ⓗ Ⓙ	4 Ⓕ Ⓖ Ⓗ Ⓙ	8 Ⓕ Ⓖ Ⓗ Ⓙ	12 Ⓕ Ⓖ Ⓗ Ⓙ Ⓚ	16 Ⓕ Ⓖ Ⓗ Ⓙ	20 Ⓕ Ⓖ Ⓗ Ⓙ
1 Ⓐ Ⓑ Ⓒ Ⓓ	5 Ⓐ Ⓑ Ⓒ Ⓓ	9 Ⓐ Ⓑ Ⓒ Ⓓ	13 Ⓐ Ⓑ Ⓒ Ⓓ Ⓔ	17 Ⓐ Ⓑ Ⓒ Ⓓ	
2 Ⓕ Ⓖ Ⓗ Ⓙ	6 Ⓕ Ⓖ Ⓗ Ⓙ	10 Ⓕ Ⓖ Ⓗ Ⓙ	14 Ⓕ Ⓖ Ⓗ Ⓙ	18 Ⓕ Ⓖ Ⓗ Ⓙ	

PART 4   STUDY SKILLS

E1 Ⓐ Ⓑ Ⓒ Ⓓ	3 Ⓐ Ⓑ Ⓒ Ⓓ	6 Ⓕ Ⓖ Ⓗ Ⓙ	9 Ⓐ Ⓑ Ⓒ Ⓓ	12 Ⓕ Ⓖ Ⓗ Ⓙ
1 Ⓐ Ⓑ Ⓒ Ⓓ	4 Ⓕ Ⓖ Ⓗ Ⓙ	7 Ⓐ Ⓑ Ⓒ Ⓓ	10 Ⓕ Ⓖ Ⓗ Ⓙ	13 Ⓐ Ⓑ Ⓒ Ⓓ
2 Ⓕ Ⓖ Ⓗ Ⓙ	5 Ⓐ Ⓑ Ⓒ Ⓓ	8 Ⓕ Ⓖ Ⓗ Ⓙ	11 Ⓐ Ⓑ Ⓒ Ⓓ	14 Ⓕ Ⓖ Ⓗ Ⓙ

Part 1   Language Mechanics

Example   Directions: Mark the answer choice for the punctuation mark that is needed in the sentence. If no punctuation mark is needed fill in the answer circle for "None".

E1

Which street should we take to get to the stadium?

   A .   **B** !   **C** ,   **D** None

---

1   Help, I spilled the whole bottle of juice

   A ?   **B** !   **C** .   **D** None

2   "Remember to bring your permission slips for the class trip" reminded the teacher.

   F ,   **G** .   **H** ;   **J** None

3   Please buy some nails tape, and a box of tacks when you go to the store.

   A .   **B** "   **C** ,   **D** None

4   The chairs are in the back yard, and the grill is in the garage.

   F ,   **G** ?   **H** :   **J** None

For numbers 5-7, read each answer. Fill in the space for the choice that has a punctuation error. If there is no mistake, fill in the fourth answer space.

5   **A**   The music show at the state
      B fair is scheduled to begin
      C at 1030 A.M. in the arena.
      D *(No mistakes)*

6   **F**   The dog was so tired
      G after the hike that he
      H fell asleep in the car.
      J *(No mistakes)*

7   **A**   Tonetta swam well but
      B Divina won the race that was held
      C at the city pool complex.
      D *(No mistakes)*

For numbers 8 and 9, read each sentence with a blank. Choose the word or words that fit best in the blank and show the correct punctuation.

8 _____ you may ride your bike to the parade on Saturday.

   F Yes
   G Yes,
   H Yes'
   J Yes;

9 Last week, my _____ and cousin went to a football game.

   A aunt, uncle,
   B aunt uncle
   C aunt uncle,
   D aunt uncle;

GO

For numbers 10-13, read each answer choice. Find the sentence that is written correctly and shows the correct capitalization and punctuation.

10 **F** The news comes on at six. The whole family watches it together.

  G I like the local news. it tells me what happened in my city.

  H Did the news come on yet. I just got here and want to watch it.

  J Sports is my favorite part of the news. My mother likes the business news

11 **A** Will you run for office in the school election asked Marion?

  B Rowena answered "I want to, but I am pretty busy already."

  C "You really should run for president?" suggested Ken.

  D Lyle added, "I am certain most of the students would vote for you."

12 **F** I read the book *the big brown dog* to my little sister.

  G I forgot my *Arithmetic Book* and couldn't study for the test.

  H Randy ordered *The Joy of Fishing* from the book store.

  J *Sea dreams* is a book about an adventure in the South Pacific.

13 **A** Caitlin, hurt her knee last week when she was working out.

  B Dr. Harrison, will I be able to play basketball next week?

  C The coach will decide who will play in the championship Janetta.

  D Only students who have good grades will be able to join the team Amanda.

For numbers 14-16, read the sentence with a blank. Mark the space beside the answer choice that fits best in the blank and has correct capitalization and punctuation.

14 We picked up _____ along the highway

  F paper, cans, and other trash,
  G paper cans, and other trash
  H paper, cans, and other trash
  J paper, cans, and, other trash

15 _____ it seem very hot to you today?

  A doesn't
  B Doesnt,
  C Doesn't
  D Does'nt

16 My parents' twentieth class reunion was held on _____ .

  F June 6, 1995
  G June 6 1995
  H June, 6 1995
  J June, 6, 1995

Choose the correct answer for number 17.

17 What is the correct abbreviation for the word *Monday*?

  A Mon,
  B Mon:
  C Mon;
  D Mon.

GO

Bettina is writing a letter to her older brother who is away at college. Read the letter and use it to do numbers 18-21.

```
Dear andy

    It's great being an only child. Mom and Dad can
    (1)
give me all their attention. Seriously, we all miss
                                (2)
you and look forward to seeing you soon?

    The school play is this weekend. You wouldn't
    (3)
believe how funny Reginas costume is. She is
                    (4)
playing a magic bird and looks hilarious. Her
                                (5)
feathers, beak, and feet are totally ridiculous.

Her acting is great, however, and even the other
(6)
people in the play clap for her.

    How is everything at college? Are you and your
    (7)                                 (8)
roommate getting along well? He seemed really nice
                                    (9)
when we met him.
```

18 At the beginning of Bettina's letter, Dear andy is best written —

F Dear Andy,
G Dear Andy
H Dear Andy.
J As it is

19 In sentence 2, soon? is best written —

A Soon!
B soon.
C soon,
D As it is

20 In sentence 3, Reginas costume is best written —

F Regina's Costume
G Reginas' costume
H Regina's costume
J As it is

21 In sentence 5, feathers, beak, and feet is best written —

A feathers beak and feet
B feathers beak, and feet
C feathers beak and feet,
D As it is

95

STOP

Example   Directions: Find the underlined part that is the simple subject of the sentence.

E1

Seven people waited on the corner for the bus.
  A   B   C   D

For number 1, choose the word or phrase that best completes the sentence.

1   Stella said she can't find _____ notebook and pen.

  A   her

  B   hers

  C   she

  D   shes

For number 2, choose the answer that is a complete and correctly written sentence.

2   F   Long lines for the rides and for the food stands.

  G   The petting zoo with animals like cows, goats, and sheep.

  H   A rodeo on Thursday night and a tractor pull on Friday night.

  J   The parking lot at the state fair was crowded with cars and trucks.

For numbers 3-5, read each answer choice. Fill in the space for the choice that has a usage error. If there is no mistake, fill in the fourth answer space.

3   A   The shoes that I bought
  B   don't fit very well. I am
  C   going to return them tomorrow.
  D   *(No mistakes)*

4   F   Me and Alinda will go
  G   to the movies on Saturday
  H   afternoon with her parents.
  J   *(No mistakes)*

5   A   A large wave knocked
  B   Brett over. He got up laughing
  C   and said it wasn't nothing.
  D   *(No mistakes)*

For number 6, find the underlined part that is the simple subject of the sentence.

6   The mayor of our town attended a meeting in Washington, DC.
       F   G   H   J

For number 7, find the underlined part that is the simple predicate (verb) of the sentence.

7   The students threw a party for their teacher.
      A   B   C   D

GO

For numbers 8-10, choose the answer that best combines the underlined sentences.

8 The driver put the turn signal on.

The driver turned right.

F The driver turned right but put the turn signal on.

G The driver put the turn signal on and turned right.

H Turning right, the driver putting the turn signal on.

J The driver, who put the turn signal on, and turned right.

9 The room was filled with children.

The children were happy.

A The room was filled with happy children.

B The room was filled and the children were happy.

C The children were happy who filled the room.

D Filled with happy children was the room.

10 The mall is new.

The mall is near my house.

The mall is very large.

F Near my house is a mall and it is very large and new.

G Large and new, the mall is near my house.

H The mall near my house is new, and the mall is very large.

J The new mall near my house is very large.

For numbers 11 and 12, choose the best way of expressing the idea.

11 **A** At our school swims my sister on the team.
  B The team at our school on which my sister swims.
  C My sister swims on the team at our school.
  D My sister at our school swims on the team.

12 **F** Please help me put out the trash, but before you go to school.
  G Please help me before you go to school put out the trash.
  H Help me before you go to school the trash to put out.
  J Before you go to school, please help me put out the trash.

Read the paragraph below. Find the best topic sentence for the paragraph.

13 _____ . She installs computer systems in doctors' offices. After learning about each doctor's practice, she decides what kind of computer and programs will be best.

   A Many doctors have computers in their offices.

   B Many exciting jobs are available in the computer field.

   C Samantha's mother went to college to become an engineer.

   D Samantha's mother has an interesting job.

Find the answer choice that best develops the topic sentence.

14   The fall is my favorite time of the year.

   F The weather is cool, but it is still warm enough to play outside. The leaves on the trees change from green to many beautiful colors.

   G Spring is nice, too. After a long, cold winter, spring brings flowers and warmer weather.

   H In October, the leaves on the trees change color. Birds fly south in the fall where they spend the winter.

   J Football is played in the fall. I like football, but soccer is my favorite sport.

Read the paragraph below. Find the sentence that does not belong in the paragraph.

15   1. The Declaration of Independence is a famous document.   2. It declared that the United States was independent from England.   3. The Declaration of Independence was adopted on July 4, 1776.   4. Each year, we have a family picnic on July 4.

   A Sentence 1

   B Sentence 2

   C Sentence 3

   D Sentence 4

Read the paragraph below. Find the sentence that best fits the blank in the paragraph.

16   The workers began by digging a large hole in the ground. _____. A mixing truck came, and the workers put concrete into the wooden forms. Two days later, they removed the forms and the foundation for our house was finished.

   F It will take about four months to build our house.

   G They start work at eight in the morning.

   H Wooden forms were placed around the edge of the hole.

   J A strong foundation is necessary when you build a house.

GO

Here is more of Bettina's letter to her older brother. Read the letter and use it to do numbers 17-20.

My Spanish class took yesterday a field trip to
(1)
the museum. There was a special showing of art from
(2)
Mexico and Central America. Mrs. Chavez only spoke
(3)
Spanish at the museum and made us do the same

thing! It was hard, but we learned a lot.
(4)
    It has taken me forever, but I finished the book
(5)
you gave me, *The Hobbit*. Mom and Dad were impressed
(6)
that I read a book that was so thick. I tried to
(7)
read at least a few pages every day. Some nights
(8)
asleep reading and with the light on. There are
(9)
three more books that follow it, and I want to read

them all.

    I have to go to school now. Study hard.
(10)

Your little sister,

Bettina

17 Sentence 1 is best written—

 A Yesterday a field trip to the museum my class took.
 B Yesterday, my Spanish class took a field trip to the museum.
 C A field trip to the museum was taken yesterday by my Spanish class.
 D To the museum yesterday my Spanish class a field trip took.

18 Which of these is *not* a sentence?

 F 2
 G 3
 H 8
 J 9

19 Which sentence could be added after sentence 4?

 A I feel that I could give a tour in Spanish now.
 B We took a bus from school to the museum.
 C I listen to a Spanish radio station at night when I study.
 D Mrs. Chavez was born in Puerto Rico.

20 In sentence 3, only spoke is best written —

 F only will speak
 G only to speak
 H only speaking
 J As it is

99

STOP

Examples   Directions: Read the directions for each section. Fill in the circle for the answer you think is correct.

E1 Find the word that is spelled correctly and fits best in the blank.

Can you please _____ this for me?

A copy
B copie
C coppy
D kopy

E2 Choose the phrase in which the underlined word is not spelled correctly.

F window sticker
G messy room
H good player
J secind place

For numbers 1-6, find the word that is spelled correctly and fits best in the blank.

1 The librarian helped me do _____ for my history project.

A reserch
B resaerch
C research
D reaserch

2 It started out as an _____ day.

F ordnary
G ordinary
H oridinary
J oridnary

3 Do you know what makes a ship _____ ?

A flote
B floate
C flot
D float

4 The players were _____ they would win.

F confident
G confadent
H confidint
J confedint

5 Lance was not _____ he was late.

A awair
B awaer
C aware
D awaire

6 Linda's _____ was lost at the airport.

F bagage
G bagige
H baggage
J baggadge

For numbers 7-10, read the phrases. Choose the phrase in which the underlined word is not spelled correctly.

7 A quick reply
    B feel helples
    C important news
    D living well

8 F patch a tire
    G pancake batter
    H wipe a dish
    J leave earley

9 A win a prize
    B group meeting
    C repare a tire
    D beautiful valley

10 F kitchen tabel
    G sign a form
    H being kind
    J tell a joke

GO

For numbers 11-13, read each answer. Fill in the space for the choice that has a spelling error. If there is no mistake, fill in the last answer space.

11
- **A** western
- **B** happy
- **C** false
- **D** teacher
- **E** *(No mistakes)*

12
- **F** joind
- **G** silly
- **H** never
- **J** garden
- **K** *(No mistakes)*

13
- **A** popular
- **B** chart
- **C** light
- **D** friendily
- **E** *(No mistakes)*

For numbers 14-16, read each phrase. One of the underlined words is not spelled correctly for the way it is used in the phrase. Fill in the space for the word that is not spelled correctly.

14
- **F** computer <u>control</u>
- **G** rare <u>stamp</u>
- **H** colorful <u>flour</u>
- **J** <u>enter</u> a room

15
- **A** <u>describe</u> an event
- **B** <u>pale</u> of water
- **C** good <u>harvest</u>
- **D** surprising <u>result</u>

16
- **F** <u>scent</u> letters
- **G** <u>carve</u> wood
- **H** <u>notice</u> something
- **J** <u>prepare</u> food

For numbers 17-20, find the underlined part that is misspelled. If all the words are spelled correctly, mark the space under <u>No mistake</u>.

17 The <u>clerk</u> spent an hour stocking the <u>shelvs</u> in the <u>supermarket</u>. <u>No mistake</u>.
       A   B   C   D

18 <u>Farmers</u> will <u>oftin</u> have to work from <u>dawn</u> to dusk. <u>No mistake</u>.
   F   G   H   J

19 Andrew <u>nerely</u> missed his <u>airplane</u> because traffic was so <u>heavy</u>. <u>No mistake</u>.
         A   B   C   D

20 We <u>skated</u> on a <u>frozen</u> pond with <u>several</u> of our friends. <u>No mistake</u>.
       F   G   H   J

Example

Directions: Study the schedule. Read the question. Mark the answer you think is correct.

SCHEDULE

8:00	Homeroom
8:30	Mathematics
9:30	English
10:30	History
11:30	Lunch
12:00	Science
2:00	Science Lab

E1

Look at the schedule on the left. In which class would you be at 10:15?

A History
B Mathematics
C Science
D English

Study the map below. Use it to do numbers 1-4.

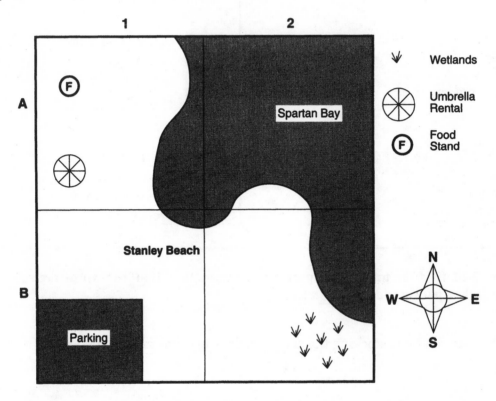

1 In which section of the map is the parking lot located?

A A-1
B A-2
C B-1
D B-2

2 Where is the food stand located?

F north of the umbrella rental
G northwest of the parking lot
H northeast of the wetlands
J south of the parking lot

3 If you walked from the parking lot to the wetlands, you would be going—

A east.
B west.
C north
D south.

4 Which section of the map is mostly water?

F B-2
G B-1
H A-1
J A-2

For numbers 5-9, choose the best answer to each question.

5 Which of these would you use to find the day of the week on which Fourth of July falls this year?

A   a dictionary
B   an encyclopedia
C   a telephone book
D   a calendar

6 What would you find in the index of a book?

F   the title of each chapter in the book and the page on which it starts
G   topics and the pages on which they are found
H   words found in the book and their meanings
J   the year the book was published and the name of the publisher

7 Where would you look to find all the different meanings for a word?

A   an almanac
B   an encyclopedia
C   a dictionary
D   a crossword puzzle

8 In which of these books would you look to find out the name of a flower you saw in a state park?

F   *Flowers in America*
G   *State Parks in America*
H   *Drying Flowers*
J   *Arranging Flowers*

9 Which of these would probably appear on a map of the United States?

A   the name of the street on which you live
B   the year the first highway in the United States was built
C   interstate highways
D   school names

For numbers 10-13, choose the word or name that would come first if the words or names were arranged in alphabetical order.

10   F   king
         G   queen
         H   moat
         J   royal

11   A   climb
         B   coming
         C   certain
         D   crayon

12   F   Lanton, Tom
         G   Rawlings, Louise
         H   Hawley, Eli
         J   Tallman, Linda

13   A   Miller, Kevin
         B   Miller, Brenda
         C   Miller, Omar
         D   Miller, Patricia

For number 14, read the sentences. Then choose the key words that should be included in research notes on the Constitution.

14 The Constitution, which sets forth the laws of the United States, became effective in March of 1789. It can only be changed by adding amendments.

F   Constitution sets forth laws; became effective; amendments
G   U.S. laws; effective in March; amended in 1789
H   U.S. Constitution; amended in 1789; changed in March by amendment
J   Constitution contains U.S. laws; effective in 1789; can be amended

STOP

Table of Contents
Math

UNIT 1   CONCEPTS
Lesson 1   Numeration

Example   **Directions:** Read and work each problem. Find the correct answer. Mark the space for your choice.

A What whole number is one greater than 9? **A** 8 **B** 10 **C** 7 **D** 11	**B** Which of these will have a remainder when it is divided by 7? **F** 14 **G** 28 **H** 22 **J** 35

Look at all the answer choices before you mark the one you think is correct.

Be sure the answer circle you fill in is the same letter as the answer you think is correct.

Practice

1 Which of these numbers is an even number and a multiple of 9?

A 36
B 39
C 27
D 45

2 Which group of numbers is in order from smallest to largest?

F 6, 24, 18, 57, 38
G 29, 11, 35, 46, 58
H 14, 21, 34, 53, 82
J 4, 12, 23, 76, 45

3 Which of these answers is the expanded numeral for 835?

A 8 + 3 + 5
B 800 + 3 + 10 + 5
C 800 + 50 + 3
D 800 + 30 + 5

4 What number goes in the box on the number line shown below?

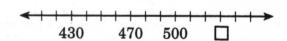

430   470   500   ☐

F 510
G 530
H 490
J 600

5 How do you write 400 + 20 + 8 as one numeral?

A 4028
B 4208
C 40,208
D 428

GO

6 Which number between 20 and 30 is both odd and a multiple of 7?

F 28

G 27

H 21

J 35

7 Which of these is another way to write ten hundreds?

A 10,000

B 10,100

C   100

D   1000

8 Which of these is less than 45 and greater than 32?

F 36

G 32

H 45

J 48

9 Which of these is the expanded numeral for 361?

A 36 + 1

B 300 + 60 + 1

C 3 + 61

D 300 + 600 + 100

10 2 hundreds and 7 ten thousands =

F 10,207

G 70,020

H   207

J 70,200

11 A builder has 100 bags of cement. It takes 30 bags of cement to make the sidewalk for a house. What is the greatest number of sidewalks the builder can make?

A 30

B 70

C   3

D   4

12 Which is the numeral for 8 thousands, 2 hundreds, 4 tens, and 9 ones?

F   8249

G 82,049

H 80,249

J   8294

13 Which of these is between 284,601 and 399,046?

A 199,601

B 399,406

C 299,046

D 284,106

14 If these numbers are put in order from greatest to least, what is the middle number?

| 200 | 350 | 250 | 400 | 300 |

F 250

G 300

H 350

J 325

Example   **Directions:** Read and work each problem. Find the correct answer.
Mark the space for your choice.

A What is the meaning of 470?

- Ⓐ 47 hundreds
- Ⓑ 4 tens and 7 ones
- Ⓒ 4 hundreds and 7 tens
- Ⓓ 4 hundreds and 7 ones

B 148 =

- Ⓕ fourteen hundred, eight
- Ⓖ one hundred forty-eight
- Ⓗ one hundred eighty-four
- Ⓙ one thousand, forty-eight

 Read each question carefully. Look for key words and numbers that will help you find the answers.

If a problem is too difficult, skip it and come back to it later.

Practice

1 Which of these numerals has a 3 in the hundreds place?

- Ⓐ 3231
- Ⓑ 3123
- Ⓒ 1233
- Ⓓ 3312

2 What number is expressed by
(2 x 1000) + (6 x 100) + (9 x 1)?

- Ⓕ 2690
- Ⓖ 2609
- Ⓗ 269
- Ⓙ 2069

3 Fifty thousand, seventy =

- Ⓐ 50,070
- Ⓑ 50,007
- Ⓒ 57,000
- Ⓓ 50,700

4 Which shape is missing from this pattern?

   ?

Ⓕ   Ⓗ

Ⓖ   Ⓙ

5 What number is missing from the sequence shown below?

| 50, 43, 36, ___ , 22, 15 |

- Ⓐ 28
- Ⓑ 30
- Ⓒ 29
- Ⓓ 33

GO

6 How many of these numbers are even?

| 3   8   14   23   87   46 |

(F) 2

(G) 3

(H) 5

(J) 6

7 Which numeral has a 9 in the thousands place?

(A) 20,519

(B) 90,125

(C) 10,925

(D) 19,025

8 What does the 7 in 3784 mean?

(F) 700

(G) 7000

(H) 7

(J) 70

9 Thomas began a small business selling bags of dried fruit. In the first week he sold 11 bags, in the second week 14 bags, and in the third week 17 bags. If this pattern continues, how many bags of fruit will he sell in the sixth week?

(A) 29

(B) 23

(C) 20

(D) 26

10 Three hundred ninety-two =

(F) 392

(G) 329

(H) 30,092

(J) 39,200

11 Which numeral has 40 ones, 5 hundreds, and 1 thousand?

(A) 1504

(B) 1405

(C) 1540

(D) 4051

12 If the pattern in the box is continued, what figure will come next?

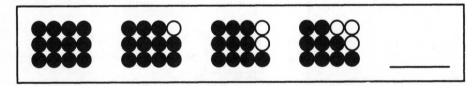

(F)

(G)

(H)

(J)

STOP

Example   **Directions:** Read and work each problem. Find the correct answer.
Mark the space for your choice.

A What is 458 rounded to the nearest ten?

   A 460

   B 450

   C 410

   D 510

B Which number sentence goes with
23 + 8 = 31?

   F 31 + 8 = 39

   G 23 + 31 = 54

   H 31 − 8 = 23

   J 23 − 8 = 15

Sometimes you won't have to compute to find the answer to a
problem. For this type of problem, it's especially important to
look for key words and numbers that will help you find the
correct answer.

Eliminate answer choices you know are wrong.

Practice

1 The ☐ stands for what number?

$$\square \times 12 = 36$$

   A 6

   B 48

   C 24

   D 3

2 Each row in the number pyramid below
equals 15. What numbers are missing from
the pyramid?

```
           15
        7     8
      4   5    ?
    ?   9   2   3
```

   F 2 and 6

   G 7 and 2

   H 6 and 1

   J 1 and 8

3 A number rounded to the nearest ten is 550.
When it is rounded to the nearest hundred,
the number becomes 600. Which of these
could it be?

   A 554

   B 545

   C 559

   D 549

4 What number goes in the box to make this
number sentence true?

$$\frac{\square}{9} = \frac{15}{27}$$

   F 15

   G 5

   H 2

   J 7

GO

5 Which of the following number facts does <u>not</u> belong to the same family or group as 40 ÷ 8 = 5?

A 8 x 5 = 40

B 5 x 8 = 40

C 40 ÷ 5 = 8

D 40 x 8 = 320

6 What should replace the ☐ in the number sentence below?

$$5 \ \square \ 7 = 35$$

F x

G ÷

H +

J –

7 The sum of two numbers is 10. Their difference is 6. What are the numbers?

A 9 and 1

B 9 and 3

C 8 and 2

D 8 and 1

8 In which of the subtraction problems below must you rename a ten as ten ones or borrow a ten?

F   17
    – 13

G   13
    – 7

H   13
    – 10

J   13
    – 3

9 Suppose you are estimating by rounding to the nearest ten. What numbers should you use to estimate 17 from 52?

A 20 and 60

B 10 and 60

C 10 and 50

D 20 and 50

10 The function table below shows "input" and "output" numbers. The rule used to change the "input" numbers to "output" numbers is shown above the table. What number completes the table?

Rule: Add 3, then multiply by 4

IN	OUT
2	20
3	24
5	?

F 28

G 32

H 23

J 36

11 Michele had $10\frac{2}{3}$ feet of wood. She used 9 feet to build shelves. Which of these shows how much wood she had left?

A $10\frac{2}{3} + 9 = \square$

B $10\frac{2}{3} \times 9 = \square$

C $10\frac{2}{3} - 9 = \square$

D $10\frac{2}{3} + 9 = \square$

STOP

Example   **Directions:** Read and work each problem. Find the correct answer. Mark the space for your choice.

A Which fraction shows how many of the shapes on the right are shaded?

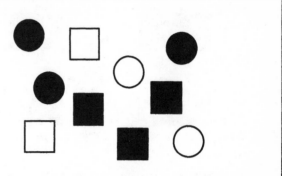

A $\frac{1}{6}$

B $\frac{3}{5}$

C $\frac{7}{10}$

D $\frac{1}{2}$

Pay close attention to the numbers in the problem and in the answer choices. If you misread even one number, you will probably choose the wrong answer.

Some problems will be easier to solve if you use scratch paper.

Practice

1 On the number line below, which arrow points most closely to 2.1?

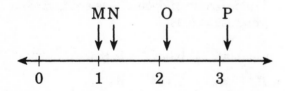

A M

B N

C O

D P

2 0.43 =

F $\frac{4}{3}$

G $\frac{430}{100}$

H $\frac{43}{10}$

J $\frac{43}{100}$

3 Which number tells how much of the figure below is shaded?

A 0.75

B 0.6

C 0.8

D 0.45

4 Which of these numbers comes between 3.68 and 3.86?

F 3.89

G 3.17

H 3.71

J 3.66

GO

5 Which two shapes have an equal portion of the blocks shaded?

1

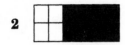
2

3

4

A 1 and 4

B 2 and 3

C 2 and 4

D 3 and 4

6 Which fraction names the greatest number?

F $\frac{4}{5}$

G $\frac{2}{3}$

H $\frac{1}{3}$

J $\frac{1}{9}$

7 Which of these has a value greater than $\frac{1}{4}$?

A $\frac{1}{8}$

B $\frac{1}{5}$

C $\frac{1}{6}$

D $\frac{1}{3}$

8 Which of these is another name for $\frac{10}{25}$?

F $\frac{1}{2}$

G $\frac{3}{8}$

H $\frac{2}{5}$

J $\frac{1}{3}$

9 What math fact do the pictures below show to be true?

 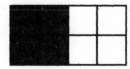

A $\frac{4}{8}$ is less than $\frac{1}{2}$

B $\frac{4}{8}$ is equal to $\frac{1}{2}$

C $\frac{4}{8}$ is greater than $\frac{1}{2}$

D $\frac{4}{8}$ is equal to $\frac{1}{4}$

10 Which of the decimals below has an 8 in the hundredths place?

F 9.348

G 8.349

H 3.894

J 4.389

11 Which group of decimals is ordered from greatest to least?

A 6.902   6.387   6.154

B 6.902   6.154   6.387

C 6.387   6.902   6.154

D 6.154   6.387   6.902

12 Which of the decimals below names the smallest number?

F 1.90

G 1.21

H 1.09

J 1.18

STOP

Examples   **Directions:** Read and work each problem. Find the correct answer. Mark the space for your choice.

E1

Which of these numerals has a 4 in the hundreds place?

A 1479

B 1974

C 4197

D 7149

E2

Which of the number sentences below is true?

F 25,610 < 25,106

G 27,543 < 27,534

H 22,902 < 22,920

J 26,824 < 26,824

---

1 Which of these is a group of odd numbers?

A 23, 39, 10, 17

B 21, 36, 7, 19

C 23, 35, 7, 13

D 22, 34, 8, 14

2 Which number fact makes this number sentence true?

$$5 + 8 = \boxed{}$$

F 8 + 5

G 8 x 5

H 13 − 8

J 8 − 5

3 What number goes in the box on the number line below?

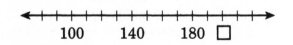

100   140   180 ☐

A 190

B 200

C 195

D 210

4 Suppose you had 15 objects and you wanted to put them into 5 boxes. How would you find out the number of objects that would fit into each box?

F divide 15 by 5

G multiply 15 by 5

H add 15 and 5

J subtract 5 from 15

5 6 x 10,000 =

A   16,000

B 610,000

C 600,000

D   60,000

6 What fraction of the shape below is shaded?

F $\frac{2}{5}$

G $\frac{5}{12}$

H $\frac{1}{3}$

J $\frac{4}{11}$

GO ▷

---

7 From the ground floor to Merrie's apartment is 32 steps. Which number sentence shows how many steps Merrie takes to go from her apartment to the ground floor and back?

A $32 - 2 = \square$

B $32 + 2 = \square$

C $32 \times 2 = \square$

D $32 \div 2 = \square$

8 If this number pattern continues, what number will come next?

10, 20, 12, 18, 14, 16, ___

F 18

G 16

H 12

J 14

9 What is another way to write 32 hundreds?

A 320

B 132

C 32,000

D 3200

10 What should replace the $\square$ in

$9 + (5 + 7) = (9 + 5) + \square$?

F 4

G 5

H 9

J 7

11 Where is the arrow pointing on the number line below?

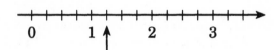

A $1\frac{1}{4}$

B $1\frac{1}{2}$

C $2\frac{3}{4}$

D $2\frac{1}{2}$

12 What would be a fast way to add the same number 10 times?

F Subtract 10 from the number

G Divide the number by 10

H Multiply the number by 10

J Add 10 to the number

13 Jonathan bought $4.89 worth of school supplies and paid for them with a $10 bill. About how much change did he get?

A $4

B $5

C $6

D $1

14 What number makes these number sentences true?

$\square \times 3 = 3$
$3 \times \square = \square \times 3$

F 11

G 0

H 10

J 1

STOP

Lesson 6   Addition

Example   **Directions:** Mark the space for the correct answer to each addition problem. Choose "None of these" if the right answer is not given.

A		A 19
	23	B 21
	+ 4	C 7
		D 28
		E None of these

B		F 146
	56 + 9 =	G 65
		H 75
		J 47
		K None of these

If the right answer is not one of the choices, mark the space for "None of these."

The answer in an addition problem is always larger than the numbers being added.

Practice

1

    66
    32
  + 21

A 120
B 109
C 91
D 119
E None of these

5

   37
 + 10

A 27
B 137
C 47
D 380
E None of these

2

  289
 + 34

F 223
G 323
H 213
J 313
K None of these

6

  $9.95
 + 4.29

F $13.34
G $5.66
H $14.24
J $14.84
K None of these

3

32 + 28 + 7 =

A 60
B 57
C 58
D 68
E None of these

7

  2007
  5281
 + 119

A 7307
B 7397
C 8407
D 7408
E None of these

4

3562 + 1200 =

F 4762
G 3512
H 3762
J 3574
K None of these

8

12 + □ = 45

F 57
G 33
H 23
J 24
K None of these

GO ⟩

9

$$3\frac{1}{5}$$
$$+\ 3\frac{1}{5}$$

A $6\frac{1}{5}$

B $6\frac{3}{5}$

C $6\frac{1}{10}$

D $7\frac{1}{10}$

E None of these

10

$$78$$
$$+\ 75$$

F 143

G 153

H 177

J 151

K None of these

11

$$\frac{1}{8} + \frac{6}{8} =$$

A $\frac{7}{16}$

B $\frac{8}{7}$

C $\frac{5}{8}$

D $\frac{7}{8}$

E None of these

12

$$4.7$$
$$+\ 0.19$$

F 40.79

G 4.719

H 4.89

J 4.51

K None of these

13

$$\frac{2}{3}$$
$$+\ 5$$

A $5\frac{2}{3}$

B $\frac{7}{3}$

C $\frac{2}{8}$

D $4\frac{1}{3}$

E None of these

14

$$7.0 + 0.24 =$$

F 72.4

G 7.24

H 70.24

J 700.24

K None of these

15

$$\frac{1}{9}$$
$$+\ \frac{4}{9}$$

A $\frac{8}{9}$

B $\frac{5}{18}$

C $\frac{1}{9}$

D $\frac{5}{9}$

E None of these

16

$$4398 + 5124 =$$

F 8422

G 8522

H 9512

J 9524

K None of these

17

$$\frac{1}{11} + \frac{3}{11} = \square$$

A $\frac{4}{11}$

B $\frac{4}{22}$

C $\frac{2}{11}$

D 4

E None of these

18

$$27 + 55 + 2 + 8 =$$

F 85

G 93

H 82

J 92

K None of these

STOP

ANSWER ROWS   9 Ⓐ Ⓑ Ⓒ Ⓓ Ⓔ   11 Ⓐ Ⓑ Ⓒ Ⓓ Ⓔ   13 Ⓐ Ⓑ Ⓒ Ⓓ Ⓔ   15 Ⓐ Ⓑ Ⓒ Ⓓ Ⓔ   17 Ⓐ Ⓑ Ⓒ Ⓓ Ⓔ
116   10 Ⓕ Ⓖ Ⓗ Ⓙ Ⓚ   12 Ⓕ Ⓖ Ⓗ Ⓙ Ⓚ   14 Ⓕ Ⓖ Ⓗ Ⓙ Ⓚ   16 Ⓕ Ⓖ Ⓗ Ⓙ Ⓚ   18 Ⓕ Ⓖ Ⓗ Ⓙ Ⓚ

Example

Directions: Mark the space for the correct answer to each subtraction problem. Choose "NG" if the right answer is not given.

A		A 25	B		F 0.29
		B 200			G 1.1
250		C 205	$0.9 - 0.2 =$		H 0.92
− 25		D 275			J 0.7
		E NG			K NG

If the right answer is not given, mark the space for "NG." This means "not given."

When you are not sure of an answer, check it by adding.

Practice

1

9.98
− 0.7

A   10.68
B   9.28
C   9.981
D   9.91
E   NG

5

201
− 82

A   283
B   219
C   118
D   111
E   NG

2

5271
− 429

F   4258
G   5700
H   5847
J   4842
K   NG

6

$22.06 − $11.96 =

F $10.10
G $47.72
H $32.68
J $37.82
K   NG

3

$2000 - 800 =$

A   2200
B   600
C   1200
D   1800
E   NG

7

$5.62 - 0.81 =$

A   6.43
B   50.6281
C   4.81
D   50.21
E   NG

4

43.2
− 2.4

F   40.2
G   45.6
H   43.44
J   41.8
K   NG

8

4450
− 2001

F   6451
G   2449
H   2495
J   2451
K   NG

GO

9

$9\frac{6}{7}$
$-\ 2\frac{2}{7}$

A $6\frac{4}{7}$
B $7\frac{3}{7}$
C $6\frac{4}{14}$
D $12\frac{1}{7}$
E NG

10

$\frac{8}{11}-\frac{3}{11}=$

F $\frac{5}{11}$
G 1
H $\frac{3}{8}$
J $\frac{4}{11}$
K NG

11

$\frac{12}{13}$
$-\ \frac{10}{13}$

A $\frac{1}{13}$
B $\frac{2}{13}$
C $\frac{3}{13}$
D $1\frac{1}{2}$
E NG

12

$\frac{8}{9}$
$-\ \frac{1}{9}$

F 1
G $\frac{5}{9}$
H $\frac{6}{9}$
J $\frac{7}{9}$
K NG

13

$22.46
$-\ 17.89$

A $4.57
B $40.35
C $4.43
D $5.57
E NG

14

798
− 176

F 613
G 622
H 864
J 781
K NG

15

8.5 − 2.1 =

A 5.4
B 10.6
C 4.6
D 6.3
E NG

16

52 − 7 =

F 35
G 44
H 45
J 59
K NG

17

834 − 612 =

A 122
B 213
C 231
D 222
E NG

18

6683
− 4047

F 2636
G 2644
H 2611
J 2614
K NG

19

5340 − 1200 =

A 4260
B 4160
C 4140
D 5540
E NG

STOP

Example

Directions: Mark the space for the correct answer to each multiplication problem. Choose "NH" if the right answer is not given.

A		A 36
		B 28
32		C 148
x 4		D 126
		E NH

B		F 47
		G 28
4 x 7 =		H 11
		J 3
		K NH

If the right answer is not given, mark the space for "NH." This means "not here."

If you are not sure which answer is correct, take your best guess and move on to the next item.

Practice

1

   30
x 5

A 350
B 35
C 180
D 150
E NH

5

4 x 45 =

A 180
B 150
C 49
D 445
E NH

2

6 x 1000 =

F 600
G 1600
H 6100
J 6000
K NH

6

   34
x 2

F 36
G 86
H 324
J 328
K NH

3

   20
x 80

A 2800
B 8200
C 16,000
D 1800
E NH

7

3 x 44 = ☐

A 344
B 47
C 132
D 122
E NH

4

7 x 309 =

F 2179
G 2163
H 379
J 316
K NH

8

   51
x 24

F 1204
G 1214
H 5124
J 1224
K NH

STOP

Example

Directions: Mark the space for the correct answer to each division problem. Choose "N" if the right answer is not given.

A		B	
2)‾20‾	Ⓐ 10 Ⓑ 8 Ⓒ 18 Ⓓ N	48 ÷ 4 =	Ⓕ 14 Ⓖ 10 R3 Ⓗ 11 Ⓙ N

You can check your answers in a division problem by multiplying your answer by either the dividend or divisor.

If the right answer is not given, mark the space for "N". This means the answer is not given.

Practice

1

639 ÷ 3 =

Ⓐ 203
Ⓑ 213
Ⓒ 21
Ⓓ N

5

6)‾5124‾

Ⓐ 921
Ⓑ 854
Ⓒ 804
Ⓓ N

2

4)‾18‾

Ⓕ 4 R2
Ⓖ 4
Ⓗ 8 R2
Ⓙ N

6

490 ÷ 7 =

Ⓕ 70
Ⓖ 700
Ⓗ 497
Ⓙ N

3

45 ÷ 5 =

Ⓐ 11
Ⓑ 225
Ⓒ 8
Ⓓ N

7

3)‾42‾

Ⓐ 126
Ⓑ 324
Ⓒ 12
Ⓓ N

4

7)‾105‾

Ⓕ 10 R3
Ⓖ 10 R5
Ⓗ 15
Ⓙ N

8

12 ÷ 4 = □

Ⓕ 48
Ⓖ 4
Ⓗ 3
Ⓙ N

STOP

Examples **Directions:** Work each problem. Mark the answer you think is correct. Choose "None of these" if the correct answer is not given.

E1		A 1.3
		B 2.7
1.2 + 1.5 =		C 0.3
		D 1.8
		E None of these

E2		F 11
		G 12
72 ÷ 8 =		H 8
		J 7
		K None of these

1

14 x 7 =

A 728
B 21
C 147
D 98
E None of these

6

$3.00
+ 0.42

F $34.20
G $30.42
H $3.24
J $2.34
K None of these

2

77
98
+ 86

F 251
G 161
H 260
J 261
K None of these

7

6)6

A 0
B 12
C 1
D 36
E None of these

3

500
− 472

A 28
B 38
C 128
D 972
E None of these

8

63
x 27

F 432
G 1701
H 90
J 1221
K None of these

4

0.8 + 0.7 =

F 1.6
G 0.78
H 1.7
J 0.87
K None of these

9

821
− 44

A 787
B 877
C 865
D 777
E None of these

5

53 − 7 =

A 60
B 46
C 47
D 23
E None of these

10

2058 + 371 =

F 2429
G 23,587
H 1687
J 20,551
K None of these GO

ANSWER ROWS
E1 Ⓐ Ⓑ Ⓒ Ⓓ Ⓔ   2 Ⓕ Ⓖ Ⓗ Ⓙ Ⓚ   5 Ⓐ Ⓑ Ⓒ Ⓓ Ⓔ   8 Ⓕ Ⓖ Ⓗ Ⓙ Ⓚ
E2 Ⓕ Ⓖ Ⓗ Ⓙ Ⓚ   3 Ⓐ Ⓑ Ⓒ Ⓓ Ⓔ   6 Ⓕ Ⓖ Ⓗ Ⓙ Ⓚ   9 Ⓐ Ⓑ Ⓒ Ⓓ Ⓔ
1 Ⓐ Ⓑ Ⓒ Ⓓ Ⓔ   4 Ⓕ Ⓖ Ⓗ Ⓙ Ⓚ   7 Ⓐ Ⓑ Ⓒ Ⓓ Ⓔ   10 Ⓕ Ⓖ Ⓗ Ⓙ Ⓚ

11

$\frac{3}{7} + \frac{2}{7} =$

   A $\frac{1}{7}$

   B $\frac{5}{7}$

   C 1

   D $\frac{5}{14}$

   E None of these

12

$4 \times 600 =$

   F 6400
   G 604
   H 2400
   J 4600
   K None of these

13

$9.3 - 8.8 =$

   A 18.1
   B 17.9
   C 0.5
   D 1.5
   E None of these

14

$8\overline{)33}$

   F 6
   G 3
   H 3 R3
   J 4 R1
   K None of these

15

$6923 - 3419 =$

   A 3514
   B 3516
   C 3504
   D 2504
   E None of these

16

$45 + 15 =$

   F 3
   G 30
   H 300
   J 13
   K None of these

17

   477
+ 248

   A 231
   B 2525
   C 726
   D 625
   E None of these

18

$\$7.62 - \$7.43 =$

   F $0.39
   G $0.31
   H $0.29
   J $0.21
   K None of these

19

   20.3
+ 2.03

   A 41.209
   B 22.33
   C 22.6
   D 23.23
   E None of these

20

$300 \div 10 =$

   F 20
   G 290
   H 200
   J 30
   K None of these

21

$\frac{9}{11}$
$- \frac{1}{11}$

   A $\frac{8}{11}$

   B $\frac{10}{11}$

   C 1

   D $\frac{11}{8}$

   E None of these

22

$21.4 - 0.7 =$

   F 20.7
   G 23.1
   H 217.4
   J 149.8
   K None of these

Lesson 11   Geometry

Example   **Directions:** Find the correct answer to each geometry problem.
Mark the space for your choice.

A Which of the figures below is a cone?

A

B

C

D

   **Read the question carefully and look for key words, numbers, and figures before you choose an answer.**

Practice

1 Which of these letters has a line of symmetry?

A **F**

B **A**

C **L**

D **R**

2 How many edges does a cube have?

F   4

G   8

H   12

J   6

3 What is the area of this shape?
(Area = length x width)

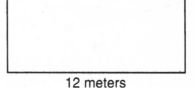

5 meters

12 meters

A   60 square meters

B   34 square meters

C   17 square meters

D   65 square meters

4 What is the perimeter of a square room if each side is 9 feet?

F   13 feet

G   16 feet

H   81 feet

J   36 feet

GO

5   How many triangles are in this figure?

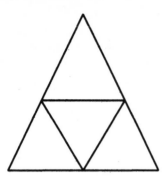

   A 10

   B 7

   C 5

   D 9

6   Which of these pairs of lines seems to be parallel?

F

G
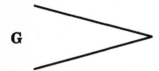

H

J
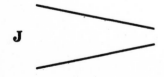

7   Which of these shapes has an area of 10 square units?

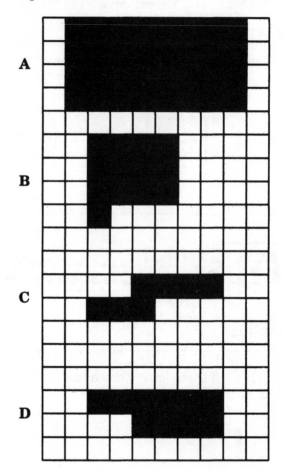

8   A drinking glass is shaped most like a —

   F rectangular prism

   G cylinder

   H cube

   J sphere

9   How many corners does a triangle have?

   A 6

   B 4

   C 3

   D 2

10 Which of these answers shows two circles inside a rectangle?

F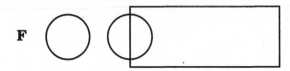

G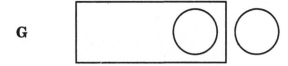

H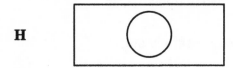

J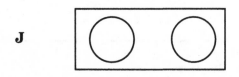

11 Which pair of shapes is congruent?

A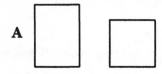

B

C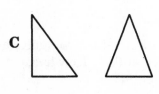

D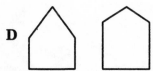

12 What is the area of this shape in square units?

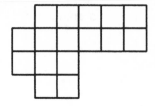

F 16

G 14

H 24

J 18

13 What is the perimeter of the figure below?

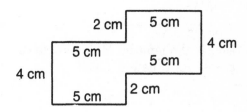

A 12 cm

B 50 cm

C 28 cm

D 32 cm

14 Which of the figures below does not show a line of symmetry?

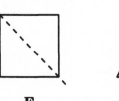

F   G

   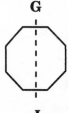

H   J

STOP

ANSWER ROWS   **10** Ⓕ Ⓖ Ⓗ Ⓙ   **12** Ⓕ Ⓖ Ⓗ Ⓙ   **14** Ⓕ Ⓖ Ⓗ Ⓙ

11 Ⓐ Ⓑ Ⓒ Ⓓ   **13** Ⓐ Ⓑ Ⓒ Ⓓ

Example   **Directions:** Find the correct answer to each measurement problem. Mark the space for your choice.

A About how long is a dollar bill? **A** 20 inches **B** 18 inches **C** 6 inches **D** 1 inch	**B** Three quarters are worth — **F** 75¢ **G** 28¢ **H** $1.00 **J** 50¢

Before you choose an answer, ask yourself, "Does this answer make sense?"

If you work on scratch paper, transfer numbers carefully and perform the correct operation.

Practice

1   What is the length of this line, to the nearest centimeter?

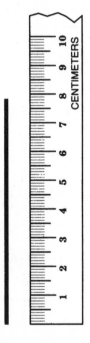

A   10 cm
B   8 cm
C   6 cm
D   5 cm

2   30 inches is —

F   equal to 3 feet
G   more than a yard
H   equal to 2 feet
J   less than a yard

3   Which of these would you probably measure in meters?

A   the height of a tree
B   the distance between two cities
C   the weight of a horse
D   the amount of medicine in a bottle

4   Deena began working at the computer at 6:15. She finished at 6:40. How long did she work at the computer?

F   35 minutes
G   40 minutes
H   60 minutes
J   25 minutes

GO

5 What temperature does this thermometer show?

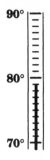

A 83°

B 90°

C 81°

D 79°

6 What time is shown on this clock?

F 40 minutes after 8

G 40 minutes to 8

H 10 minutes to 8

J 40 minutes to 7

7 Nick is in a bicycle race that will take about an hour to finish. Which measurement unit will probably be used to show the length of the race?

A meters

B kilometers

C millimeters

D centimeters

8 Look at the calendar below. What is the date of the last Friday in November?

NOVEMBER						
S	M	T	W	T	F	S
		1	2	3	4	5
6	7	8	9	10	11	12
13	14	15	16	17	18	19
20	21	22	23	24	25	26
27	28	29	30			

F November 25

G November 26

H November 30

J November 27

9 Suppose you had 2 quarters, 2 dimes, a nickel, and 4 pennies. Which of these could you buy?

A a burger for 79¢

B a slice of pizza for $1.29

C a six-pack of soda for $2.39

D a taco for 89¢

10 How many hours are in two days?

F 12 hours

G 24 hours

H 30 hours

J 48 hours

11 How many centimeters are in one meter?

A 1000

B 100

C 10

D 10,000

GO

12   If it is 7:30 now, what time will it be in 3 hours?

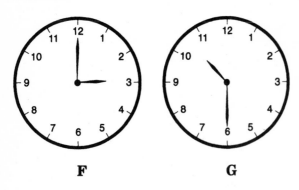

F   G

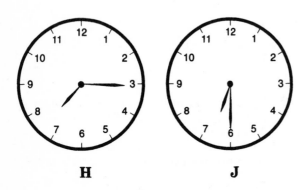

H   J

13   What is the value of 2 dollars, 3 quarters, 3 dimes, and 4 nickels?

A $3.25

B $2.75

C $2.25

D $3.05

14   Suppose you were going to a movie that started at 4:00. If you leave the house at 3:25, how much time do you have before the movie starts?

F   25 minutes

G   45 minutes

H   35 minutes

J   1 hour and 25 minutes

15   Which of these digital clocks shows 20 minutes before seven o'clock?

A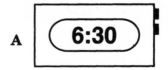

B

C

D

16   How do you write 54 cents as part of a dollar?

F   54$

G   ¢54

H   54¢

J $.54

17   Vivian wants to buy a toy that costs $1.39. She has the coins below. How much more does she need?

A $1.04

B   74¢

C   65¢

D $1.05

GO

18 Which of these is worth more than $1.50?

   F 40 nickels

   G 5 quarters

   H 15 dimes

   J 5 quarters and 2 dimes

19 Which clock shows that the time is 20 after 1?

      A   **B**

      C   **D**

20 The container below holds one quart of liquid. How many containers would it take to equal 1 gallon?

   F 8

   G 4

   H 2

   J 12

21 Dylan has 7 nickels. He wants to buy a ball that costs 60¢. How much more money does he need?

   A 44¢

   B 62¢

   C 42¢

   D 25¢

22 Suppose you wanted to mail a regular letter to a friend. About how much do you think the letter would weigh?

   F 1 pound

   G 8 pounds

   H 1 ounce

   J 8 ounces

23 Felicia's desk is between 1 and 2 meters long. About how many centimeters long might her desk be?

   A 150 cm

   B 250 cm

   C 50 cm

   D 500 cm

24 What temperature will this thermometer show if the temperature drops 25°?

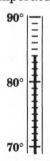

   F 39°

   G 59°

   H 51°

   J 24°

STOP

Example   **Directions:** Find the correct answer to each problem. Mark the space for your choice.

A   There are 12 eggs in a dozen. Which number sentence shows how many eggs are in 3 dozen?

ⓐ 12 ÷ 3 = ☐

ⓑ 12 - 3 = ☐

ⓒ 12 + 3 = ☐

ⓓ 12 x 3 = ☐

B   Bo's turtles weigh 12 ounces, 10 ounces, and 20 ounces. What is their average weight?

Ⓕ 15 ounces

Ⓖ 11 ounces

Ⓗ 42 ounces

Ⓙ Not Given

Be sure to consider all the answer choices. Rework a problem if your answer is not one of the choices.

Choose "Not Given" only if you are sure the right answer is not one of the choices.

Practice

1   Hiking shoes usually cost $49. This week they are on sale for $7 less than the regular price. What is the sale price of athletic shoes?

ⓐ $49 x $7 = ☐

ⓑ $49 + $7 = ☐

ⓒ $49 - $7 = ☐

ⓓ $49 ÷ $7 = ☐

2   A group of 32 students went to a basketball game. They went in 4 vans that held the same number of students. How many students were in each van?

Ⓕ 32 ÷ 4 = ☐

Ⓖ 32 x 4 = ☐

Ⓗ 32 - 4 = ☐

Ⓙ 32 + 4 = ☐

3   Sue picked 84 apples and her brother Manny picked 78 apples. How many apples did they pick altogether?

ⓐ 184

ⓑ 178

ⓒ 152

ⓓ 162

4   How much will one apple cost if 5 apples cost $1.00?

Ⓕ $1.05

Ⓖ $.94

Ⓗ $.20

Ⓙ $.95

5   Which of the following directions could be used to move from zero to point X on the graph below?

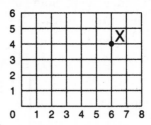

ⓐ Go up 4 units and right 6 units.

ⓑ Go up 5 units.

ⓒ Go right 7 units.

ⓓ Go right 5 units and up 7 units.

GO ▷

---

6   A case of soda contains 24 bottles. If you put 15 bottles in the refrigerator, how many bottles would remain in the case?

Ⓕ   11

Ⓖ   19

Ⓗ   8

Ⓙ   Not Given

7   Which of these events is most likely to happen?

Ⓐ   A friend from school will call you on the telephone.

Ⓑ   You will find a box of money on the street.

Ⓒ   A helicopter will land in your back yard and a movie star will get out.

Ⓓ   You will go to the store and find that everything is free.

8   The local paper has 48 pages. Norm read 31 pages. How many pages of the paper does Norm have left to read?

Ⓕ   ☐ - 31 = 48

Ⓖ   48 + 31 = ☐

Ⓗ   31 - ☐ = 48

Ⓙ   48 - ☐ = 31

9   A yard is surrounded by 400 yards of fence. It took Lynne 8 days to paint the whole fence. Her father asked her how much fence she painted each day. Which number sentence can Lynne use to figure out how much fence she painted in a day?

Ⓐ   400 x 8 = ☐

Ⓑ   400 ÷ 8 = ☐

Ⓒ   400 - 8 = ☐

Ⓓ   400 + 8 = ☐

10   Antonia bought 5 cans of corn and 3 cans of peas. Each can contains 16 ounces. Which number sentence shows the total weight of what Antonia bought?

Ⓕ   (5 - 3) x 16 = ☐

Ⓖ   3 x 5 x 16 = ☐

Ⓗ   (3 x 5) x 16 = ☐

Ⓙ   (5 + 3) x 16 = ☐

11   A box contains 5 red crayons, 3 green crayons, and 2 blue crayons. If you reach into the box without looking, what is the probability of picking a green crayon?

Ⓐ $\frac{3}{10}$

Ⓑ $\frac{3}{5}$

Ⓒ $\frac{1}{3}$

Ⓓ   Not Given

12   It takes a train 3 hours to go from Town A to Town B. What else do you need to know to figure the average speed of the train?

Ⓕ   The direction the train traveled

Ⓖ   The time the train arrived at Town B

Ⓗ   The time the train left Town A

Ⓙ   The distance between the towns

13   Five students want to find their average height in inches. Their heights are 54 inches, 56 inches, 52 inches, 57 inches, and 53 inches. How would you find the average height of the students?

Ⓐ   Add the heights and multiply by 5.

Ⓑ   Add the heights and divide by 5.

Ⓒ   Add the heights and divide by the number of inches in 1 foot.

Ⓓ   Multiply the heights and divide by the number of inches in 1 foot.

GO

The graph below shows the length of four hiking trails. Use the graph to answer questions 14 through 16.

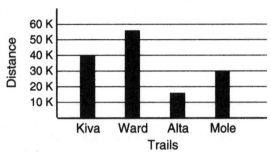

Length of Hiking Trails

14 If you wanted to hike a trail that was less than 20 kilometers long, which trail would you choose?

Ⓕ Kiva

Ⓖ Ward

Ⓗ Alta

Ⓙ Mole

15 If you hiked 15 kilometers a day, how long would it take you to hike the Mole trail?

Ⓐ 2 days

Ⓑ 1 day

Ⓒ 3 days

Ⓓ 15 days

16 During the spring, the members of a school outdoor club hiked all four trails. How many kilometers altogether did they hike?

Ⓕ 150 kilometers

Ⓖ 135 kilometers

Ⓗ 100 kilometers

Ⓙ 140 kilometers

17 The Student and Parent Club in a school is raising money for new computers. They need $3000 dollars and have already collected $1400. How much more money do they have to raise?

Ⓐ $4400

Ⓑ $3000

Ⓒ $1500

Ⓓ Not Given

18 The list below shows the equipment the club wants to buy and its cost. Based on the information on the list, how much will be spent on software?

4 computers	$2000
1 printer	$250
software	?

Ⓕ $1000

Ⓖ $2500

Ⓗ $750

Ⓙ Not Given

19 The computers will be available for 5 days each week for 6 hours a day. What is the total number of hours per week the computers will be available?

Ⓐ 30 hours

Ⓑ 11 hours

Ⓒ 35 hours

Ⓓ Not Given

20 Each student will spend 20 minutes at the computer. How many students will be able to use a computer in one hour?

Ⓕ 2

Ⓖ 3

Ⓗ 1

Ⓙ Not Given

GO

The graph below shows how many buttons were on the clothing of five students in a class. Use the graph to answer questions 21 through 23.

NUMBER OF BUTTONS

Jason	⦿⦿⦿⦿⦿⦿
Pat	⦿⦿
Nancy	⦿⦿⦿⦿
Paul	⦿⦿⦿⦿⦿
Shirley	⦿⦿⦿

⦿ = 4 buttons

21 How many buttons were on Nancy's clothes?

Ⓐ 4
Ⓑ 8
Ⓒ 16
Ⓓ Not Given

22 Which student had the fewest buttons?

Ⓕ Pat
Ⓖ Paul
Ⓗ Shirley
Ⓙ Jason

23 How many buttons did the student with the most buttons have?

Ⓐ 6
Ⓑ 24
Ⓒ 10
Ⓓ 46

24 Suppose you knew the weight of a package of meat and the price per pound of the meat. Which of these questions could you not answer?

Ⓕ What is the price of the meat when it is on sale for 10¢ a pound less?
Ⓖ What is the price of 5 pounds of meat?
Ⓗ What is the price of the package of meat?
Ⓙ What is the price of the same meat at another store?

The table below shows the number of visitors to a museum in a week. Use the table below to answer questions 25 and 26.

NUMBER OF VISITORS

	8 AM	10 AM	NOON	2 PM
MONDAY	12	14	23	32
TUESDAY	14	14	24	32
WEDNESDAY	15	16	23	36
THURSDAY	17	12	25	34
FRIDAY	10	14	28	31
SATURDAY	17	19	30	42
SUNDAY	19	22	31	45

25 What was the total number of visitors to the museum on Sunday?

Ⓐ 119
Ⓑ 117
Ⓒ 108
Ⓓ Not Given

26 What was the increase in visitors from 8 AM to 2 PM on Wednesday?

Ⓕ 21
Ⓖ 11
Ⓗ 36
Ⓙ 51

STOP

Examples   **Directions:** Read and work each problem. Find the correct answer. Mark the space for your choice.

E1

In the fourth grade class there are 14 girls and 11 boys. What is the total number of students in the class?

A $14 \div 11 = \square$
B $14 + 11 = \square$
C $14 - 11 = \square$
D $14 \times 11 = \square$

E2

Which of the shapes below is most like a rectangular prism?

F ice cream cone

G egg

H basketball

J shoe box

---

1 It takes 5 minutes to clean a car in an automatic car wash. How long will it take to clean 7 cars?

A $7 \div 5 = \square$
B $7 - 5 = \square$
C $5 \times 7 = \square$
D $7 + 5 = \square$

2 A piece of pipe is 120 centimeters long. If you cut off 49 centimeters, how much pipe will be left?

F $\square \times 49 = 120$
G $\square \div 49 = 120$
H $49 - \square = 120$
J $120 - \square = 49$

3 When Iris visited the park, she counted 96 birds in a 4-hour period. What was the average number of birds she counted in an hour?

A 24
B 29
C 92
D 100

4 A wrestler weights 165 pounds. He wants to weigh 156 pounds. How much weight must he lose?

F 6 pounds
G 11 pounds
H 9 pounds
J 8 pounds

5 A room is 4 yards wide by 5 yards long. Carpet costs $22 a yard, and it takes about 6 hours to install. The cost of padding to go under the carpet is $5 a yard. Which information is <u>not</u> needed to find out how much it will cost to install carpet in the room?

A The cost of carpet

B The time needed to install it

C The length of the room

D The width of a room

6 What is the perimeter of the figure below?

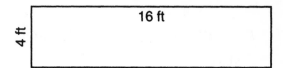

F 40 ft

G 20 ft

H 64 ft

J 24 ft

7 Which group of coins below is worth the most money?

A 7 nickels and 7 dimes

B 7 dimes and 3 nickels

C 3 quarters and 6 dimes

D 5 quarters and 3 pennies

GO ⟩

ANSWER ROWS   **E1** Ⓐ Ⓑ Ⓒ Ⓓ   **1** Ⓐ Ⓑ Ⓒ Ⓓ   **3** Ⓐ Ⓑ Ⓒ Ⓓ   **5** Ⓐ Ⓑ Ⓒ Ⓓ   **7** Ⓐ Ⓑ Ⓒ Ⓓ

E2 Ⓕ Ⓖ Ⓗ Ⓙ   **2** Ⓕ Ⓖ Ⓗ Ⓙ   **4** Ⓕ Ⓖ Ⓗ Ⓙ   **6** Ⓕ Ⓖ Ⓗ Ⓙ

The chart below shows the cost of different automobile services. Use the chart to answer numbers 8 through 10.

Automobile Services		
Service	Price for Small Car	Price for Large Car
Oil Change	$12.95	$14.95
Wash only	$5.00	$5.00
Wax only	$20.00	$25.00
Wash and wax	$22.50	$27.50
Rotate tires	$8.00	$8.00
Tune-up	$39.95	$49.95
Winterize	$19.95	$24.95

8 What is the most expensive service?

   F Tune-up for large car

   G Tune-up for small car

   H Wash and wax for large car

   J Winterize for small car

9 How much does it cost to winterize a small car?

   A $24.95

   B $19.95

   C $39.95

   D $12.95

10 Which of these statements is true?

   F It costs more to wash a small car than a large car.

   G It costs the same to change the oil in a small car and in a large car.

   H It is $10 more expensive to tune-up a large car than a small car.

   J It is $10 more expensive to wax a large car than a small car.

11 The irrigation canal between the towns of High Point and Lawrence is 27 miles long. The cost of building the canal was $10,000 per mile. What was the total cost of the canal?

   A $370,000

   B $117,000

   C $270,000

   D $127,000

12 Vern measured the depth of the canal in 3 spots and found it to be 6 feet, 10 feet, and 11 feet. What was the average depth he found?

   F 8 feet

   G 7 feet

   H 10 feet

   J Not Given

13 One of the bridges across the canal is 7 meters above the water level. The water under the bridge is 3.5 meters deep. How many meters is it from the bridge to the bottom of the canal?

   A 10.5 meters

   B 3.5 meters

   C 4.5 meters

   D Not Given

14 Barges sometimes use the canal to carry grain from High Point to Lawrence. The barges travel at the rate of 6 miles an hour. How long will it take a barge to travel the 27 miles from High Point to Lawrence?

   F Exactly 3 hours

   G Less than 4 hours

   H More than 5 hours

   J Between 4 and 5 hours

GO ⟩

15 Which line segment seems to be congruent to $\overline{XY}$?

A

B

C

D

16 About how long is this feather?

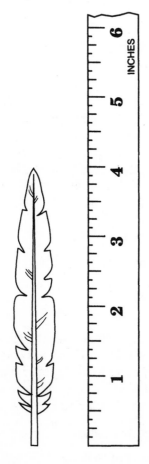

F 6 inches

G 3 inches

H 4 inches

J 5 inches

17 A business recently hired 23 new workers. They had 58 workers before. How many workers does the business have now?

A 81

B 83

C 71

D 35

18 How would you get from Point M to Point N on the graph below?

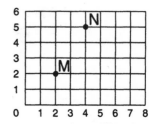

F Go up 3 units and right 4 units

G Go right 3 units and up 2 units

H Go up 3 units and left 2 units

J Go up 3 units and right 2 units

19 What temperature will this thermometer show if the temperature rises 12°?

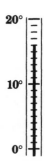

A 22°

B 28°

C 18°

D 26°

GO

The graph below shows the number of new houses built in a town over a 6 year period. Study the chart, then do numbers 20 through 23.

Number of Houses Built

20 In which year were 20 houses built?

F 1989

G 1991

H 1992

J 1987

21 How many houses were built in 1988?

A 65

B 70

C 55

D 60

22 How many more houses were built in 1987 than in 1989?

F 60

G 10

H 80

J 20

23 Between which two years was the change in the number of houses built the greatest?

A 1991 and 1992

B 1990 and 1991

C 1989 and 1990

D 1987 and 1988

24 Karen bought a pen for 72¢ and paid for it with a dollar bill. Which group of coins did she receive as change?

25 Which of these letters has a line of symmetry?

A **Q**

B **P**

C **N**

D **M**

GO

26 What is the area of this shape in square units?

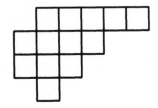

F 12 square units

G 11 square units

H 10 square units

J 13 square units

27 What day of the week is February 22?

FEBRUARY						
S	M	T	W	T	F	S
			1	2	3	4	5
6	7	8	9	10	11	12
13	14	15	16	17	18	19
20	21	22	23	24	25	26
27	28					

A Wednesday

B Monday

C Tuesday

D Friday

28 Bernie and his family drove $1\frac{1}{2}$ days to the lake for vacation. They stayed at the lake for 3 days and then drove home again. How many days in all were they away?

F 6 days

G $4\frac{1}{2}$ days

H $3\frac{1}{2}$ days

J 5 days

29 If it is 5:00 now, what time was it 20 minutes ago?

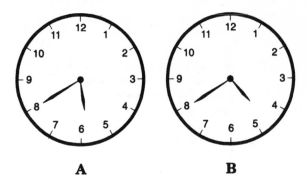

A   B

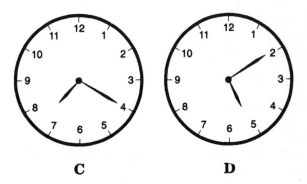

C   D

30 Suppose you knew the number of people on a bus and their ages. Which of these questions could you answer?

F What is the average age of the people on the bus?

G What is the birthday of the oldest person on the bus?

H How many people got off the bus on the first stop?

J How many people have the same birthday?

31 Which of these is the greatest volume?

A 17 cups

B 8 quarts

C 17 pints

D 3 gallons

STOP

ANSWER ROWS   **26** Ⓕ Ⓖ Ⓗ Ⓙ   **28** Ⓕ Ⓖ Ⓗ Ⓙ   **30** Ⓕ Ⓖ Ⓗ Ⓙ

27 Ⓐ Ⓑ Ⓒ Ⓓ   **29** Ⓐ Ⓑ Ⓒ Ⓓ   **31** Ⓐ Ⓑ Ⓒ Ⓓ   NUMBER RIGHT_____

Name and Answer Sheet

To the Student:

These tests will give you a chance to put the tips you have learned to work.

A few last reminders...

- Be sure you understand all the directions before you begin each test. You may ask the teacher questions about the directions if you do not understand them.
- Work as quickly as you can during each test.
- When you change an answer, be sure to erase your first mark completely.

- You can guess at an answer or skip difficult items and go back to them later.
- Use the tips you have learned whenever you can.
- It is OK to be a little nervous. You may even do better.

Now that you have completed the lessons in this unit, you are on your way to scoring high!

STUDENT'S NAME		SCHOOL
LAST	FIRST	MI	
			TEACHER
			FEMALE ○ MALE ○

BIRTHDATE

MONTH	DAY	YEAR
JAN ○	⓪ ⓪	⓪
FEB ○	① ①	①
MAR ○	② ②	②
APR ○	③ ③	③
MAY ○	④	④
JUN ○	⑤	⑤ ⑤
JUL ○	⑥	⑥ ⑥
AUG ○	⑦	⑦ ⑦
SEP ○	⑧	⑧ ⑧
OCT ○	⑨	⑨ ⑨
NOV ○		
DEC ○		

GRADE

② ③ ④ ⑤ ⑥ ⑦

139

PART 1   CONCEPTS

E1 Ⓐ Ⓑ Ⓒ Ⓓ	4 Ⓕ Ⓖ Ⓗ Ⓙ	9 Ⓐ Ⓑ Ⓒ Ⓓ	14 Ⓕ Ⓖ Ⓗ Ⓙ	19 Ⓐ Ⓑ Ⓒ Ⓓ
E2 Ⓕ Ⓖ Ⓗ Ⓙ	5 Ⓐ Ⓑ Ⓒ Ⓓ	10 Ⓕ Ⓖ Ⓗ Ⓙ	15 Ⓐ Ⓑ Ⓒ Ⓓ	20 Ⓕ Ⓖ Ⓗ Ⓙ
1 Ⓐ Ⓑ Ⓒ Ⓓ	6 Ⓕ Ⓖ Ⓗ Ⓙ	11 Ⓐ Ⓑ Ⓒ Ⓓ	16 Ⓕ Ⓖ Ⓗ Ⓙ	21 Ⓐ Ⓑ Ⓒ Ⓓ
2 Ⓕ Ⓖ Ⓗ Ⓙ	7 Ⓐ Ⓑ Ⓒ Ⓓ	12 Ⓕ Ⓖ Ⓗ Ⓙ	17 Ⓐ Ⓑ Ⓒ Ⓓ	22 Ⓕ Ⓖ Ⓗ Ⓙ
3 Ⓐ Ⓑ Ⓒ Ⓓ	8 Ⓕ Ⓖ Ⓗ Ⓙ	13 Ⓐ Ⓑ Ⓒ Ⓓ	18 Ⓕ Ⓖ Ⓗ Ⓙ	23 Ⓐ Ⓑ Ⓒ Ⓓ

PART 2   COMPUTATION

E1 Ⓐ Ⓑ Ⓒ Ⓓ Ⓔ	3 Ⓐ Ⓑ Ⓒ Ⓓ Ⓔ	7 Ⓐ Ⓑ Ⓒ Ⓓ Ⓔ	11 Ⓐ Ⓑ Ⓒ Ⓓ Ⓔ	15 Ⓐ Ⓑ Ⓒ Ⓓ Ⓔ	19 Ⓐ Ⓑ Ⓒ Ⓓ Ⓔ
E2 Ⓕ Ⓖ Ⓗ Ⓙ Ⓚ	4 Ⓕ Ⓖ Ⓗ Ⓙ Ⓚ	8 Ⓕ Ⓖ Ⓗ Ⓙ Ⓚ	12 Ⓕ Ⓖ Ⓗ Ⓙ Ⓚ	16 Ⓕ Ⓖ Ⓗ Ⓙ Ⓚ	20 Ⓕ Ⓖ Ⓗ Ⓙ Ⓚ
1 Ⓐ Ⓑ Ⓒ Ⓓ Ⓔ	5 Ⓐ Ⓑ Ⓒ Ⓓ Ⓔ	9 Ⓐ Ⓑ Ⓒ Ⓓ Ⓔ	13 Ⓐ Ⓑ Ⓒ Ⓓ Ⓔ	17 Ⓐ Ⓑ Ⓒ Ⓓ Ⓔ	21 Ⓐ Ⓑ Ⓒ Ⓓ Ⓔ
2 Ⓕ Ⓖ Ⓗ Ⓙ Ⓚ	6 Ⓕ Ⓖ Ⓗ Ⓙ Ⓚ	10 Ⓕ Ⓖ Ⓗ Ⓙ Ⓚ	14 Ⓕ Ⓖ Ⓗ Ⓙ Ⓚ	18 Ⓕ Ⓖ Ⓗ Ⓙ Ⓚ	22 Ⓕ Ⓖ Ⓗ Ⓙ Ⓚ

PART 3   APPLICATIONS

E1 Ⓐ Ⓑ Ⓒ Ⓓ	5 Ⓐ Ⓑ Ⓒ Ⓓ	11 Ⓐ Ⓑ Ⓒ Ⓓ	17 Ⓐ Ⓑ Ⓒ Ⓓ	22 Ⓕ Ⓖ Ⓗ Ⓙ	26 Ⓕ Ⓖ Ⓗ Ⓙ
E2 Ⓕ Ⓖ Ⓗ Ⓙ	6 Ⓕ Ⓖ Ⓗ Ⓙ	12 Ⓕ Ⓖ Ⓗ Ⓙ	18 Ⓕ Ⓖ Ⓗ Ⓙ	23 Ⓐ Ⓑ Ⓒ Ⓓ	27 Ⓐ Ⓑ Ⓒ Ⓓ
1 Ⓐ Ⓑ Ⓒ Ⓓ	7 Ⓐ Ⓑ Ⓒ Ⓓ	13 Ⓐ Ⓑ Ⓒ Ⓓ	19 Ⓐ Ⓑ Ⓒ Ⓓ	24 Ⓕ Ⓖ Ⓗ Ⓙ	28 Ⓕ Ⓖ Ⓗ Ⓙ
2 Ⓕ Ⓖ Ⓗ Ⓙ	8 Ⓕ Ⓖ Ⓗ Ⓙ	14 Ⓕ Ⓖ Ⓗ Ⓙ	20 Ⓕ Ⓖ Ⓗ Ⓙ	25 Ⓐ Ⓑ Ⓒ Ⓓ	29 Ⓐ Ⓑ Ⓒ Ⓓ
3 Ⓐ Ⓑ Ⓒ Ⓓ	9 Ⓐ Ⓑ Ⓒ Ⓓ	15 Ⓐ Ⓑ Ⓒ Ⓓ	21 Ⓐ Ⓑ Ⓒ Ⓓ		
4 Ⓕ Ⓖ Ⓗ Ⓙ	10 Ⓕ Ⓖ Ⓗ Ⓙ	16 Ⓕ Ⓖ Ⓗ Ⓙ			

Part 1   Concepts

Examples   **Directions:** Read each question. Find the correct answer. Mark the space for your choice.

E1

Which of these is less than 70 and greater than 58?

A 54

B 69

C 57

D 77

E2

Eight thousand, two hundred nine =

F   8029

G 800,209

H   8290

J   8209

---

1 What number goes in the box on the number line below?

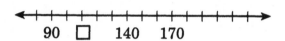

90   ☐   140   170

A 110

B 130

C 120

D 100

2 How much of the shape below is shaded?

F 0.3

G 0.312

H 0.25

J 0.4

3 What is 1783 rounded to the nearest hundred?

A 1700

B 1780

C 1800

D 1790

4 Which group of numbers is ordered from largest to smallest?

F 472, 381, 205, 367

G 176, 97, 185, 44

H 274, 301, 283, 61

J 173, 120, 85, 42

5 Which fraction shows how many of the tops below have stripes?

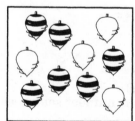

A $\frac{3}{5}$

B $\frac{1}{10}$

C $\frac{1}{6}$

D $\frac{6}{4}$

6 What number is missing from the sequence shown below?

81, 77, ___ , 69, 65, 61

F 70

G 73

H 75

J 76

GO

7 In the table below, "input" numbers are changed to "output" numbers. The rule used to change the numbers is shown above the table. What number completes the table?

Rule: Multiply by 2, then add 5

Input	Output
3	11
5	15
10	25
14	?

A 35

B 33

C 34

D 29

8 Which of these numbers has a 9 in the tenths place?

F 3.914

G 9.143

H 1.493

J 4.139

9 Which of the number sentences below is true?

A 5577 > 5775

B 3017 > 3027

C 2746 > 2981

D 1983 > 1947

10 Which number fact makes this number sentence true?

$$9 - 2 = \boxed{}$$

F 9 + 2

G 2 − 9

H 3 + 4

J 4 − 3

11 How do you write 200 + 90 + 1 as one numeral?

A 20,091

B 2091

C 200,901

D 291

12 If these numbers are put in order from least to greatest, what is the middle number?

180 300 140 220 260

F 180

G 260

H 220

J 300

13 Which of these is less than $\frac{2}{3}$?

A $\frac{3}{4}$

B $\frac{3}{10}$

C $\frac{4}{5}$

D $\frac{3}{2}$

14 Twenty four thousand, six hundred eight =

F 2468

G 24,608

H 240,608

J 24,680

15 Which number sentence goes with 14 − 8 = 6?

A 8 + 6 = 14

B 8 − 6 = 2

C 14 + 8 = 22

D 20 − 6 = 14

GO

16   Raj bought a basketball for $28.59 and a football for $19.95. About how much did he spend in all?

F $45

G $40

H $50

J $55

17   What number makes these number sentences true?

☐ x 4 = 8

☐ x ☐ = 4 x 1

A   1

B   2

C   0

D   4

18   What does the 4 in 14,207 mean?

F   400

G   40

H   40,000

J   4000

19   Which group contains only even numbers?

A   542, 760, 316, 928

B   254, 607, 361, 289

C   706, 136, 425, 928

D   928, 316, 542, 607

20   3 tens, 9 thousands, and 7 hundreds =

F   9703

G   9730

H   97,030

J   3970

21   On the number line below, which arrow is pointing most closely to $3\frac{1}{8}$?

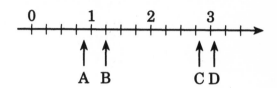

A   A

B   B

C   C

D   D

22   Which shape is missing from this pattern?

 F

 G

 H

J

23   What symbol makes this number sentence true?

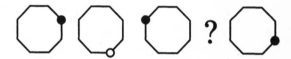

$$64 \ \square \ 16 = 4$$

A   +

B   −

C   +

D   x

143

STOP

Examples　**Directions:** Read and work each problem. Find the correct answer. Mark the space for your choice. Choose "None of these" if the correct answer is not given.

E1

$0.24
+ 0.39

A $0.53
B $0.63
C $0.15
D $0.55
E None of these

E2

$54 \div 6 = \square$

F 48
G 60
H 7
J 8
K None of these

1

$37 + 53 =$

A 100
B 110
C 89
D 90
E None of these

6

9
+ 371

F 3719
G 370
H 9371
J 362
K None of these

2

$4.38
+ 4.84

F $9.22
G $8.22
H $0.54
J $8.67
K None of these

7

$6\overline{)1212}$

A 22
B 1218
C 202
D 200 R6
E None of these

3

22.6
− 8.7

A 12.9
B 13.9
C 14.1
D 31.1
E None of these

8

51
× 4

F 204
G 240
H 47
J 55
K None of these

4

$278 + 20 + 109 =$

F 408
G 587
H 387
J 409
K None of these

9

$\frac{5}{10} + \frac{3}{10} =$

A $\frac{2}{10}$
B $\frac{3}{10}$
C $\frac{3}{5}$
D $\frac{8}{20}$
E None of these

5

$\frac{2}{9} - \frac{1}{9} =$

A $\frac{1}{2}$
B $\frac{1}{9}$
C $\frac{3}{18}$
D $\frac{1}{2}$
E None of these

10

$40\overline{)1640}$

F 400
G 410
H 44
J 41
K None of these

GO

11

$\frac{1}{3} - \frac{1}{3} = \square$

A $\frac{1}{6}$
B 0
C $\frac{2}{3}$
D $\frac{2}{6}$
E None of these

12

$8 \times 3 \times 3 =$

F 72
G 86
H 2
J 14
K None of these

13

$178 + 322 + 509 =$

A 1009
B 929
C 831
D 1777
E None of these

14

$5\overline{)85}$

F 19 R3
G 17 R3
H 19
J 18
K None of these

15

$\begin{array}{r} \frac{7}{8} \\ + \frac{1}{8} \\ \hline \end{array}$

A $\frac{5}{8}$
B 1
C $1\frac{3}{8}$
D 2
E None of these

16

$\frac{1}{7} + \frac{2}{7} = \square$

F $\frac{1}{7}$
G $\frac{3}{14}$
H $1\frac{2}{7}$
J $\frac{3}{7}$
K None of these

17

$3\overline{)218}$

A 72 R2
B 73
C 70 R8
D 72
E None of these

18

$844 - 447 =$

F 1291
G 807
H 397
J 403
K None of these

19

$\begin{array}{r} 141 \\ \times \quad 8 \\ \hline \end{array}$

A 848
B 149
C 1131
D 1121
E None of these

20

$14 \div 2 = \square$

F 6
G 5 R2
H 12
J 7
K None of these

21

$\begin{array}{r} \frac{4}{9} \\ + \frac{4}{9} \\ \hline \end{array}$

A $1\frac{1}{9}$
B $\frac{8}{9}$
C 1
D $\frac{9}{8}$
E None of these

22

$0.9 + 0.2 =$

F 0.92
G 0.29
H 1.1
J 1.01
K None of these

145

STOP

Examples   Directions: Read and work each problem. Find the correct answer. Mark the space for your choice.

E1

The Green family's electric bill in September was $35.74. In October, the bill was $8.19 more. Which number sentence shows how much the electric bill was in October?

A $35.74 + $8.19 = ☐
B $35.74 - $8.19 = ☐
C $35.74 x $8.19 = ☐
D $35.74 ÷ $8.19 = ☐

E2

What is the average height of three evergreen trees that are 21 feet, 25 feet, and 20 feet tall?

F 24 feet

G 26 feet

H 66 feet

J Not Given

---

1 If one pound of bananas cost 19¢, how much would 8 pounds cost? Mark the number sentence you would use to solve this problem.

A 19¢ ÷ 8 = ☐
B 19¢ - 8 = ☐
C 19¢ x 8 = ☐
D 19¢ + 8 = ☐

2 Toby's mother drove her car 193 miles and stopped for gas. Her entire trip was going to be 345 miles. How many more miles does she have to drive?

F ☐ x 193 = 345
G ☐ ÷ 193 = 345
H 345 - ☐ = 193
J 193 - ☐ = 345

3 A building has six floors with the same number of apartments on each floor. There are 54 apartments in the building. How many apartments are on the fourth floor?

A   9
B   54
C   63
D 324

4 In a factory with 37 workers, each person made three radios. How many radios did the workers make in all?

F 121
G   34
H   40
J 111

5 There are 24 hours in a day. Linda sleeps an average of 8 hours a day. How many hours does she not sleep?

A 24
B 16
C 32
D   3

6 In a grocery bag there are 5 cans of tomato sauce, 4 cans of beans, and 9 cans of olives. All the cans are the same size. If you reached into the bag without looking and picked out a can, what is the probability of picking a can of olives?

F $\frac{1}{2}$

G $\frac{1}{9}$

H $\frac{9}{1}$

J $\frac{1}{18}$

7 How many centimeters are in 5 meters?

A   0.5

B   50

C   5000

D   500

8 Which of these objects is <u>not</u> shaped like a sphere?

F a baseball

G a golf ball

H a tennis ball

J a football

9 Which of these is the same as 9:45?

A 15 minutes after nine

B 15 minutes to ten

C 45 minutes after ten

D 45 minutes to nine

GO

10 Which of these shapes has an area of 12 square units?

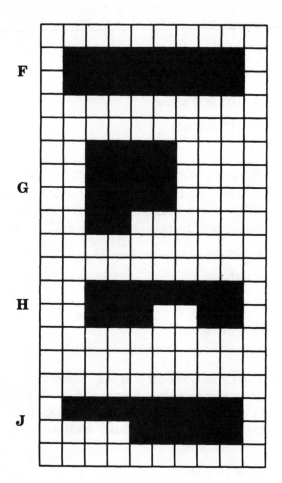

11 How many minutes are in 5 hours?

A 300

B   30

C 120

D   29

12 What is the value of these coins?

F $.60

G $.41

H $.49

J $.51

The graph below shows the cost of a ticket to the movies in five different cities. Use the graph to answer questions 13 through 16.

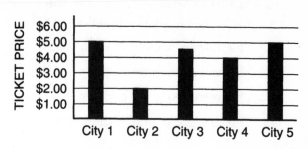

13 Which city has the cheapest movie tickets?

A City 5

B City 4

C City 2

D City 1

14 Which ticket price is found in more than one city?

F $4.00

G $10.00

H $2.00

J Not Given

15 How much more does it cost to buy a movie ticket in City 1 than in City 2?

A $5.00

B $3.00

C $2.00

D $4.00

16 Suppose you and 4 friends went to the movie in City 4. How much would you pay in all for your tickets?

F $20.00

G $4.00

H $16.00

J Not Given

147

GO

17 Suppose you knew the total cost of a bag of groceries, how much the bag weighed in pounds, and the number of items in the bag. Using this information, which of the questions below could you <u>not</u> answer?

A The average weight of each item

B The cost of each item

C The average cost of each item

D The cost per pound of the items

The graph below shows the number of glasses of water Cliff drank on five days. Study the graph, then answer questions 18 and 19.

Glasses of Water

Monday	🥛🥛🥛🥛
Tuesday	🥛🥛🥛🥛🥛🥛🥛
Wednesday	🥛🥛🥛🥛🥛🥛
Thursday	🥛🥛🥛🥛🥛🥛
Friday	🥛🥛🥛🥛🥛

18 Cliff's goal was to drink 8 glasses of water a day. On which days did he reach his goal?

F Wednesday and Friday

G Tuesday and Wednesday

H Tuesday and Thursday

J Monday and Friday

19 What was the total number of glasses of water Cliff drank during the 5 days?

A 27 glasses

B 32 glasses

C 31 glasses

D 28 glasses

20 The town of Corbett is holding its yearly Harvest Festival. Part of the event is a 10 kilometer fun run. How many meters long is the race?

F 10,000 meters

G 1000 meters

H 100,000 meters

J 100 meters

21 The entry fee for the race is $8, and all the money raised will be used for a new park. If 385 runners enter the race, how much money will be raised for the park?

A $3858

B $2480

C $393

D $3080

22 The Chili Cook-off will take place on Saturday morning. There will be 45 people in the Cook-off, and they will make 135 pounds of chili. How much chili will each person make?

F 4 pounds

G 3 pounds

H 90 pounds

J 185 pounds

23 The art sale will take place in the town square, and volunteers will build a fence around the square. The picture below shows the size of the town square. How much fence will they build?

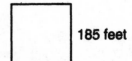

185 feet

A 4185 feet

B 1854 feet

C 740 feet

D 46 feet

GO

24 Which of the following directions could be used to move from zero to point P on the graph below?

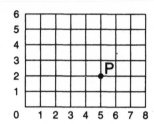

F Go over 4 units and up 3 units

G Go over 2 units and up 5 units

H Go over 5 units and up 3 units

J Go over 5 units and up 2 units

25 Which clock shows that the time is 5 minutes after 11?

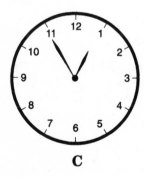

26 48 inches is the same as —

F 4 yards

G 3 feet

H 4 feet

J 1 yard

27 Suppose the temperature was 48°. What would it be if the temperature rose 15°?

A 73°

B 63°

C 33°

D 99°

28 Look at the calendar below. Suppose you had a test on April 15 and got the results back two days later. What day of the week would you get the results back?

APRIL						
S	M	T	W	T	F	S
	1	2	3	4	5	6
7	8	9	10	11	12	13
14	15	16	17	18	19	20
21	22	23	24	25	26	27
28	29	30				

F Wednesday

G Monday

H Friday

J Thursday

29 Look at the letters below. Which one does <u>not</u> have a line of symmetry?

A **O**

B **T**

C **G**

D **X**

149

STOP

Answer Keys

Answer Keys						
	1	A	31	B	19	D
	2	J	32	F	20	H
Reading	3	B	33	D	Lesson 11-pgs.34-42	
Unit 1,	4	G	34	H	A	C
Vocabulary	5	C	35	B	1	D
Lesson 1-pg.13	6	F	Unit 2, Reading		2	H
A	C	Lesson 6-pg.18		Comprehension	3	C
B	H	A	C	Lesson 8-pg.23	4	F
1	B	B	F	A	B	5	B
2	J	1	C	1	D	6	F
3	C	2	F	2	F	7	C
4	F	3	B	3	C	8	F
5	D	4	J	4	J	9	D
6	G	5	D	Lesson 9-pgs.24-27		10	F
7	A	6	H	A	B	11	D
8	G	Lesson 7-pgs.19-22		1	D	12	H
Lesson 2-pg.14	E1	D	2	G	13	B
A	D	E2	H	3	D	14	H
B	H	1	C	4	H	15	A
1	A	2	J	5	B	16	G
2	G	3	C	6	F	17	D
3	D	4	G	7	C	18	G
4	H	5	A	8	F	19	C
5	C	6	H	9	B	20	G
6	G	7	D	10	J	21	D
7	A	8	G	11	A	22	H
Lesson 3-pg.15	9	C	12	G	23	C
A	A	10	G	13	C	24	F
B	J	11	B	Lesson 10-pgs.28-33		25	C
1	C	12	H	A	B	26	G
2	G	13	D	1	B	27	B
3	D	14	F	2	F	28	H
4	F	15	B	3	A	29	A
5	C	16	F	4	H	Test Practice	
6	G	17	B	5	B	Part 1-pgs.45-48	
7	A	18	J	6	J	E1	D
8	J	19	C	7	A	E2	F
Lesson 4-pg.16	20	F	8	F	1	B
A	A	21	C	9	D	2	F
B	G	22	J	10	H	3	A
1	B	23	C	11	B	4	J
2	J	24	H	12	G	5	B
3	A	25	C	13	C	6	H
4	J	26	J	14	J	7	D
5	A	27	C	15	C	8	F
Lesson 5-pg.17	28	H	16	G	9	A
A	B	29	B	17	A	10	J
B	F	30	J	18	G	11	C

#	Ans.
12	G
13	A
14	J
15	C
16	G
17	B
18	F
19	D
20	G
21	D
22	G
23	C
24	J
25	A
26	F
27	C
28	H
29	D
30	F
31	D
32	H
33	B
34	J
35	A

Test Practice
Part 2-pgs.49-57

#	Ans.
A	C
1	A
2	H
3	C
4	J
5	B
6	H
7	A
8	G
9	A
10	J
11	B
12	F
13	B
14	J
15	A
16	G
17	C
18	J
19	C
20	F
21	B
22	F
23	C
24	G
25	A
26	G
27	D

Language
Unit 1, Language Mechanics
Lesson 1-pgs.59-60

#	Ans.
A	C
B	J
1	B
2	F
3	C
4	H
5	D
6	F
7	A
8	H
9	A
10	J
11	B
12	G
13	C
14	G
15	D
16	H

Lesson 2-pgs.61-63

#	Ans.
A	C
B	J
1	A
2	J
3	B
4	H
5	D
6	G
7	B
8	F
9	D
10	G
11	C
12	F
13	D
14	G
15	D
16	F
17	A
18	H
19	B
20	J

Lesson 3-pgs.64-67

#	Ans.
E1	C
1	A
2	J
3	C
4	G
5	C
6	J
7	A
8	G
9	B
10	F
11	B
12	J
13	C
14	H
15	A
16	J
17	B
18	H
19	D
20	G
21	A
22	J
23	B
24	F
25	C
26	H
27	B
28	F
29	D

Unit 2, Language Expressions
Lesson 4-pgs.68-70

#	Ans.
A	D
B	F
1	B
2	H
3	A
4	J
5	B
6	G
7	C
8	F
9	C
10	J
11	B
12	F
13	A
14	J
15	C
16	G
17	C
18	F
19	B
20	G

Lesson 5-pgs.71-73

#	Ans.
A	A
B	H
C	C
1	A
2	H
3	B
4	H
5	B
6	H
7	B
8	J
9	B
10	H
11	C
12	J
13	C
14	G
15	D

Lesson 6-pgs.74-77

#	Ans.
A	D
1	A
2	H
3	B
4	H
5	D
6	F
7	C
8	G
9	A
10	J
11	A
12	G
13	B
14	H

Lesson 7-pgs.78-81

#	Ans.
E1	B
1	D
2	H
3	D
4	G
5	C
6	F
7	C
8	H
9	A
10	G
11	A
12	J
13	C
14	F
15	D
16	G
17	D
18	G
19	B
20	H

Unit 3, Spelling
Lesson 8-pgs.82-83

#	Ans.
A	C

B	F	9	C	5	C	12	H
1	D	**Lesson 11-pgs.88-90**		6	F	13	B
2	J	E1	B	7	B	14	J
3	B	E2	H	8	G	**Math**	
4	H	1	A	9	A	**Unit 1, Concepts**	
5	A	2	J	10	J	**Lesson 1-pgs.105-106**	
6	J	3	D	11	C	A	B
7	A	4	H	12	J	B	H
8	G	5	D	13	D	1	A
9	E	6	G	14	F	2	H
10	J	7	A	15	D	3	D
11	A	8	G	16	H	4	G
12	H	9	A	17	B	5	D
13	D	10	J	18	H	6	H
14	G	11	C	19	A	7	D
15	D	12	J	20	J	8	F
16	F	13	D	**Test Practice**		9	B
17	A	14	F	**Part 3-pgs.100-101**		10	J
18	G	15	B	E1	A	11	C
Lesson 9-pgs.84-85		16	J	E2	J	12	F
E1	D	17	A	1	C	13	C
E2	H	**Unit 5, Test Practice**		2	G	14	G
1	C	**Part 1-pgs.93-95**		3	D	**Lesson 2-pgs.107-108**	
2	F	E1	D	4	F	A	C
3	D	1	B	5	C	B	G
4	G	2	F	6	H	1	D
5	D	3	C	7	B	2	G
6	F	4	J	8	J	3	A
7	C	5	C	9	C	4	H
8	G	6	J	10	F	5	C
9	B	7	A	11	E	6	G
10	F	8	G	12	F	7	D
11	D	9	A	13	D	8	F
12	K	10	F	14	H	9	D
13	A	11	D	15	B	10	F
14	H	12	H	16	F	11	C
15	C	13	B	17	B	12	H
16	F	14	H	18	G	**Lesson 3-pgs.109-110**	
17	C	15	C	19	A	A	A
18	J	16	F	20	J	B	H
19	C	17	D	**Test Practice**		1	D
20	F	18	F	**Part 4-pgs.102-103**		2	H
Unit 4, Study Skills		19	B	E1	D	3	A
Lesson 10-pgs.86-87		20	H	1	C	4	G
A	C	21	D	2	F	5	D
1	D	**Test Practice**		3	A	6	F
2	F	**Part 2-pgs.96-99**		4	J	7	C
3	C	E1	B	5	D	8	G
4	G	1	A	6	G	9	D
5	B	2	J	7	C	10	G
6	G	3	D	8	F	11	C
7	A	4	F	9	C	**Lesson 4-pgs.111-112**	
8	J			10	F	A	B
				11	C	1	C

2	J	A	E	8	G	18	F
3	A	B	J	9	D	19	D
4	H	1	B	10	F	20	G
5	B	2	J	11	B	21	D
6	F	3	C	12	H	22	H
7	D	4	K	13	C	23	A
8	H	5	E	14	J	24	G
9	B	6	F	15	C		

Lesson 5-pgs.113-114 (column 1)
Lesson 8-pg.119 (column 2)
Unit 3, Applications (column 3)
Lesson 13-pgs.130-133 (column 4)

Column 1
2	J
3	A
4	H
5	B
6	F
7	D
8	H
9	B
10	J
11	A
12	H

Lesson 5-pgs.113-114

E1	A
E2	H
1	C
2	F
3	B
4	F
5	D
6	H
7	C
8	G
9	D
10	J
11	A
12	H
13	B
14	J

Unit 2, Computation

Lesson 6-pgs.115-116

A	E
B	G
1	D
2	G
3	E
4	F
5	C
6	H
7	E
8	G
9	E
10	G
11	D
12	H
13	A
14	G
15	D
16	K
17	A
18	J

Lesson 7-pgs.117-118

Column 2
A	E
B	J
1	B
2	J
3	C
4	K
5	E
6	F
7	C
8	G
9	E
10	F
11	B
12	J
13	A
14	G
15	E
16	H
17	D
18	F
19	C

Lesson 8-pg.119

A	E
B	G
1	D
2	J
3	E
4	G
5	A
6	K
7	C
8	J

Lesson 9-pg.120

A	A
B	J
1	B
2	F
3	D
4	H
5	B
6	F
7	D
8	H

Lesson 10-pgs.121-122

E1	B
E2	K
1	D
2	J
3	A
4	K
5	B
6	K
7	C

Column 3
8	G
9	D
10	F
11	B
12	H
13	C
14	J
15	C
16	F
17	E
18	K
19	B
20	J
21	A
22	F

Unit 3, Applications

Lesson 11-pgs.123-125

A	D
1	B
2	H
3	A
4	J
5	C
6	F
7	D
8	G
9	C
10	J
11	B
12	F
13	D
14	H

Lesson 12-pgs.126-129

A	C
B	F
1	B
2	J
3	A
4	J
5	D
6	H
7	B
8	F
9	A
10	J
11	B
12	G
13	A
14	H
15	B
16	J
17	B

Column 4
18	F
19	D
20	G
21	D
22	H
23	A
24	G

Lesson 13-pgs.130-133

A	D
B	J
1	C
2	F
3	D
4	H
5	A
6	J
7	A
8	J
9	B
10	J
11	A
12	J
13	B
14	H
15	A
16	J
17	D
18	H
19	A
20	G
21	C
22	F
23	B
24	J
25	B
26	F

Lesson 14-pgs.134-138

E1	B
E2	J
1	C
2	J
3	A
4	H
5	B
6	F
7	C
8	F
9	B
10	H
11	C
12	J

13	A	23	C	14	J
14	J	Test Practice		15	B
15	B	Part 2-pgs.-144-145		16	F
16	H	El	B	17	B
17	A	E2	K	18	H
18	J	1	D	19	B
19	B	2	F	20	F
20	G	3	B	21	D
21	A	4	K	22	G
22	J	5	B	23	C
23	C	6	K	24	J
24	F	7	C	25	A
25	D	8	F	26	H
26	J	9	E	27	B
27	C	10	J	28	F
28	F	11	B	29	C
29	B	12	F		
30	F	13	A		
31	D	14	K		

Unit 4, Test
Practice
Part 1-pgs.-141-143

El	B	15	B	
E2	J	16	J	
1	A	17	A	
2	H	18	H	
3	C	19	E	
4	J	20	J	
5	A	21	B	
6	G	22	H	
7	B			

Unit 4, Test Practice
Part 3-pgs.146-149

8	F	El	A	
9	D	E2	J	
10	H	1	C	
11	D	2	H	
12	H	3	A	
13	B	4	J	
14	G	5	B	
15	A	6	F	
16	H	7	D	
17	B	8	J	
18	J	9	B	
19	A	10	H	
20	G	11	A	
21	D	12	J	
22	F	13	C	

Reading Progress Chart

Circle your score for each lesson. Connect your scores to see how well you are doing.

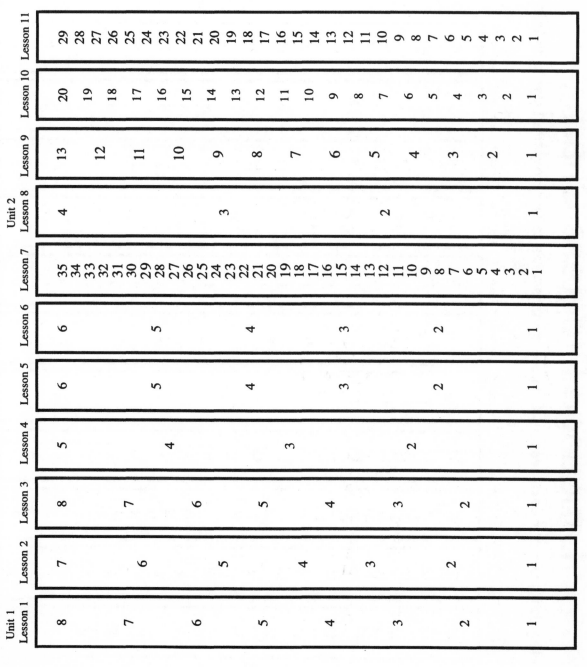

Unit 1							Unit 2			
Lesson 1	Lesson 2	Lesson 3	Lesson 4	Lesson 5	Lesson 6	Lesson 7	Lesson 8	Lesson 9	Lesson 10	Lesson 11
8	7	8	5	6	6	35	4	13	20	29
						34			19	28
7	6	7	4	5	5	33		12	18	27
						32			17	26
6	5	6		4	4	31	3	11	16	25
			3			30			15	24
5	4	5		3	3	29		10	14	23
						28			13	22
4	3	4	2	2	2	27	2	9	12	21
						26			11	20
3	2	3		1	1	25		8	10	19
			1			24			9	18
2		2				23		7	8	17
	1					22			7	16
1		1				21	1	6	6	15
						20			5	14
						19		5	4	13
						18			3	12
						17		4	2	11
						16			1	10
						15		3		9
						14				8
						13		2		7
						12				6
						11		1		5
						10				4
						9				3
						8				2
						7				1
						6				
						5				
						4				
						3				
						2				
						1				

155

Language Progress Chart

Circle your score for each lesson. Connect your scores to see how well you are doing.

Unit 1 Lesson 1	Lesson 2	Lesson 3	Unit 2 Lesson 4	Lesson 5	Lesson 6	Lesson 7	Unit 3 Lesson 8	Lesson 9	Unit 4 Lesson 10	Lesson 11
16	20	29	20	15	14	20	18	20	9	17
15	19	28	19	14	13	19	17	19		16
14	18	27	18	13	12	18	16	18	8	15
13	17	26	17	12	11	17	15	17		14
12	16	25	16	11	10	16	14	16	7	13
		24								
11	15	23	15			15	13	15		12
		22							6	
11	14	21	14	10	9	14	12	14		11
10	13	20	13			13	11	13		
		19								10
	12	18	12	9	8	12	10	12	5	
		17								9
9	11	16	11	8	7	11	9	11		
		15								8
8	10	14	10	7	6	10	8	10	4	7
	9	13	9			9		9		
7		12		6	5		7			6
	8	11	8			8		8		
6		10		5	4	7	6	7	3	5
5	7	9	7			6	5	6		
	6	8	6	4	3	5	4	5		4
4	5	7	5	3		4		4	2	3
3	4	6	4		2		3	3		
	3	5	3	2		3				2
2		4					2	2		
	2	3	2			2				
		2								
1	1	1	1	1	1	1	1	1	1	1

156

Math Progress Chart

Circle your score for each lesson. Connect your scores to see how well you are doing.

Unit 1					Unit 2					Unit 3			
Lesson 1	Lesson 2	Lesson 3	Lesson 4	Lesson 5	Lesson 6	Lesson 7	Lesson 8	Lesson 9	Lesson 10	Lesson 11	Lesson 12	Lesson 13	Lesson 14
14	12	11	12	14	18	19	8	8	22	14	24	26	31
13	11	10	11	13	17	18			21	13	23	25	30
12	10	9	10	12	16	17	7	7	20	12	22	24	29
11	9	8	9	11	15	16			19	11	21	23	28
10	8	7	8	10	14	15	6	6	18	10	20	22	27
9	7	6	7	9	13	14			17		19	21	26
8	6	5	6	8	12	13	5	5	16	9	18	20	25
7	5	4	5	7	11	12			15	8	17	19	24
6	4	3	4	6	10	11	4	4	14	7	16	18	23
5	3	2	3	5	9	10			13	6	15	17	22
4	2	1	2	4	8	9	3	3	12	5	14	16	21
3	1		1	3	7	8			11	4	13	15	20
2				2	6	7	2	2	10	3	12	14	19
1				1	5	6			9	2	11	13	18
					4	5	1	1	8	1	10	12	17
					3	4			7		9	11	16
					2	3			6		8	10	15
					1	2			5		7	9	14
						1			4		6	8	13
									3		5	7	12
									2		4	6	11
									1		3	5	10
											2	4	9
											1	3	8
												2	7
												1	6
													5
													4
													3
													2
													1

157